Camping New Mexico

Help Us Keep This Guide Up to Date

Every effort has been made by the author and editors to make this guide as accurate and useful as possible. However, many things can change after a guide is published—regulations change, techniques evolve, facilities come under new management, etc.

We would appreciate hearing from you concerning your experiences with this guide and how you feel it could be improved and kept up to date. While we may not be able to respond to all comments and suggestions, we'll take them to heart, and we'll also make certain to share them with the author. Please send your comments and suggestions to the following address:

FalconGuides
Reader Response/Editorial Department
246 Goose Lane
Guilford, CT 06437

Or you may e-mail us at: editorial@falcon.com
Thanks for your input, and happy camping!

Camping New Mexico

A Comprehensive Guide to Public Tent and RV Campgrounds

Second Edition

Melinda Crow

GUILFORD, CONNECTICUT
HELENA, MONTANA

An imprint of Rowman and Littlefield

Distributed by NATIONAL BOOK NETWORK

Copyright © 2015 by Rowman & Littlefield
Falcon, FalconGuides, and Outfit Your Mind are registered trademarks of Rowman & Littlefield.

Maps by Daniel Lloyd © Rowman & Littlefield

Photos by Melinda Crow unless otherwise noted.

British Library Cataloguing in Publication Information Available

Library of Congress Cataloging-in-Publication Data

Crow, Melinda.
  Camping New Mexico : a comprehensive guide to public tent and RV campgrounds / Melinda Crow.
– Second Edition.
     pages cm. – (A Falcon guide)
  "Distributed by NATIONAL BOOK NETWORK"–T.p. verso.
  ISBN 978-1-4930-0610-6 (paperback : alk. paper) – ISBN 978-1-4930-1479-8 (e-book) 1. Camping–New Mexico–Guidebooks. 2. Camp sites, facilities, etc.–New Mexico–Guidebooks. 3. New Mexico–Guidebooks.
I. Title.
  GV191.42.N6C76 2015
  796.5409789–dc23
                                        2015011348

♾™ The paper used in this publication meets the minimum requirements of American National Standard for Information Sciences—Permanence of Paper for Printed Library Materials, ANSI/NISO Z39.48-1992.

Contents

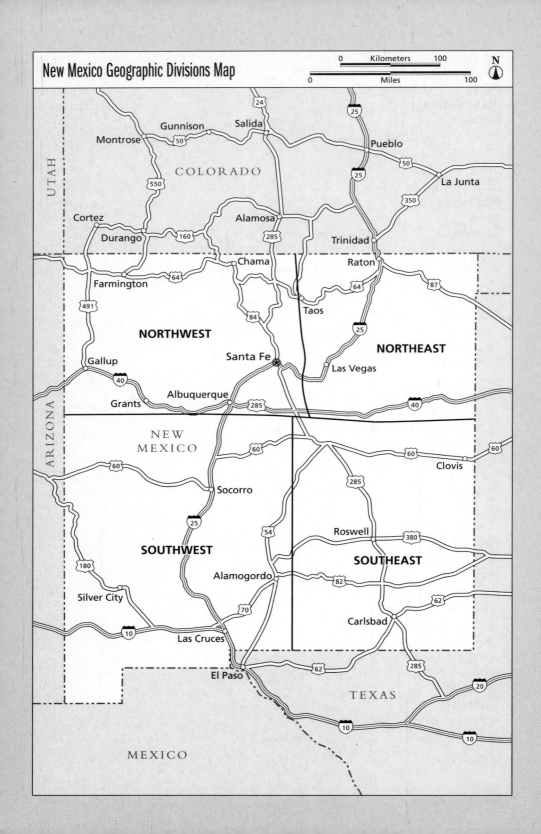

Acknowledgments

It was my pleasure during the research phase of this book to have met many wonderful people on the road. Camaraderie with fellow campers, camp hosts, and park rangers is often the highlight of my work. Without the valuable input of dedicated Forest Service personnel statewide, the content of the book would be found to be quite lacking. This was perhaps the most difficult book I have written. The reasons are many, but suffice it to say that without the undying support of my husband Gary and daughter Alyssa, completion would have been impossible. For all the fast food, for all the lonely hours while I hammered at the keyboard, and for giving me the freedom and encouragement to chase my rainbows, I thank you.

Introduction

New Mexico holds the key to my heart. The rugged landscape, with its ineffaceable contrast between desert and mountain, whispers sweet words to my soul. My goal in writing this book is to share with you the places that I love most.

The information in the front of the book should help familiarize you with the state, its inhabitants, and its camping choices. This book lists only public camping facilities. There are privately owned commercial campgrounds throughout the state, many of which are outstanding. But public camping remains the predominant choice of campers in New Mexico, perhaps because the opportunities are so wide-ranging. Also, only organized camping areas are described here. Backcountry camping is possible in many of the national forests and wilderness areas throughout the state. Be sure to check with rangers regarding restrictions and conditions.

For organizational purposes, I divide the state into four main regions and then into areas that contain camping choices. I give a brief description of each campground and provide contact information, should you wish to know more. The At-a-Glance tables for each area are designed to help you narrow the choices. Each campground description gives you the information you need to plan your trip. There's nothing more disheartening than arriving at a campground with fishing gear ready, only to learn that the nearest stream is 5 miles away. Elevations and facilities are listed as well. Rather than provide exact fees, which change frequently, the descriptions and tables provide you with a fee range, using symbols that are standard throughout the book. These ranges are based on 2014 fees and are subject to change. Many campgrounds have restrictions regarding the number of people, camping units, and vehicles per campsite. Be sure to check with the appropriate agency for specifics.

The information in this book is accurate at the time of publication, but because camping facilities change frequently, future accuracy cannot be guaranteed.

Since 1970, *New Mexico Magazine* has run a feature called "One of Our Fifty is Missing," which contains humorous examples of how the rest of the country often forgets New Mexico. I think the real reason the state is overlooked is because New Mexico is difficult to compare to the other forty-nine states. It has an isolated beauty that places it on a plane all its own. May your travels to the Land of Enchantment be all that you wish for. The road begins here.

New Mexico Wildlife

The wildlife population in the state is as diverse as the terrain. Since camping here puts you in their habitat, it is wise to educate yourself about the local fauna.

Snakes. Diamondback rattlesnakes are perhaps the creature most feared by people traveling in the southwestern United States. The rattler can be found in all regions of New Mexico, with the greatest concentrations found at elevations below 7,000 feet. Contrary to popular belief, the rattlesnake does not love extremely hot weather. In fact, its level of activity peaks at around 80 to 85 degrees F. For campers, this means morning or evening hikes are the time to use the most care. If a hike takes you through grassy or brushy areas, a walking stick or broom handle is a useful defense against snakes. Prod the brush before every step. While camping in areas likely to be inhabited by snakes, make a habit of checking shoes and sleeping bags for unwanted visitors.

Bears. The only species of bear remaining in New Mexico is the black bear. These bears are either black or light cinnamon in color. Among the New Mexico bears, there are two distinct levels of sensitivity to humans. Backcountry bears range far from population centers and are quite timid in the presence of humans. They are experts at keeping out of sight unless they wish to be seen. Frontcountry bears are those that have been desensitized to humans and are in fact more likely to come into populated areas looking for a meal than to forage in the wild. Sweet treats found in coolers and garbage cans become addicting. This segment of the bear population is growing as humans push into previously undeveloped areas of the state. Front-country bears create a nuisance in many camping areas, but unprovoked attacks on humans are rare. Still, there are things you need to know when camping in their neighborhood.

- Follow all posted regulations concerning bears.
- Bears in New Mexico can and do open car doors, so store all food and food containers inside your trunk where possible. This includes canned food, beverages, pet food, coolers, and water containers.
- Store all cooking utensils in the same manner. This includes coffee pots, stoves, silverware, and dishes, no matter how clean you think they are.
- Do not bring food, cosmetics, or other toiletries into your tent or pop-up camper. Eliminate everything that has an odor.
- Do not sleep in the same clothes you cook in. Change into clean clothes and store cooking clothes in the same way you store food.
- Immediately dispose of all trash in dumpsters or bear-proof containers.
- Hiking at dusk or dawn increases your chances of encountering a bear.
- Use extra caution when hiking in places with limited visibility, such as bends in the trail.
- Make sure children and pets stay within your sight at all times.

If you encounter a bear, either in your campsite or on the trail, both you and your children need to know how to react. The old advice of playing dead applies only to the worst-case scenario in which you are actually attacked. Your goal is to avoid this by giving the bear a way out of the confrontation.

- Stay calm. Leave the area if the bear has not detected you.
- If detected, stop and slowly back away while facing the bear, without making

direct eye contact. Give the bear plenty of space to escape; step off the trail if necessary. Remember that a charge is not an attack; startled bears may attempt to bluff.

- Speak softly to the bear.
- Never run! Always walk away. Running may trigger the bear's predatory instinct to give chase.

The national forest rangers are the best source of information regarding bear habits in the areas in which you plan to camp. For further reading, a good choice is Falcon's *Bear Aware,* by Bill Schneider.

Friendly Fauna

Now that you've read all the scary stuff and may be considering vacationing elsewhere, here's the good news. New Mexico has a vast and varied population of birds and mammals that can greatly enhance your camping trip. Take a pair of binoculars, a good field guide that includes drawings of tracks, and your sense of adventure. The list of animals you might see includes deer, elk, chipmunks, squirrels, opossums, coyotes, foxes, raccoons, gophers, beavers, and rabbits. In the skies, look for hummingbirds, jays, owls, and bats, to name a few.

A word of caution is necessary here. Never leave food out for any of these creatures. The reasons are many, but the best is simply to lessen our human impact on nature so that future generations can continue to enjoy its wild legacy.

New Mexico Camping Choices

Public camping choices in the state are quite varied, both in level of development and the terrain encompassed. There are campgrounds for those seeking comforts such as electricity, as well as more primitive camps with little or no development. And while there are variations, generalizations can be made about campgrounds offered by each of the governing agencies in the state. The following descriptions can help you decide where to begin your search for that perfect spot to hang your hammock.

State Parks. New Mexico's state parks are premier showcases of the state's culture, history, landscape, and recreational opportunities. If there's a large body of water involved, expect to find the New Mexico Parks Department in charge. In general, camping facilities at the state parks are a step above what you'll find at other campgrounds. Look for electrical hookups, dump stations, hot showers, and other amenities like marinas and visitor centers.

Most of the state parks operate year-round and offer hiking trails for visitors of all fitness levels. Ice fishing and wildlife watching are popular outdoor activities during the off-season. State park camping fees are slightly higher than those at campgrounds maintained by other agencies. However, annual passes are available for those who spend considerable time camping at the parks in a given year.

It's tempting to feed the friendly wildlife like these ground squirrels.

You can expect well-designed and well-maintained facilities at all parks.

For more information:
New Mexico State Parks
1220 S. St. Francis Dr.
Santa Fe, NM 87505
(505) 476-3355 or (888) NMPARKS
www.emnrd.state.nm.us/SPD
Reservations: (877) 664-7787; http://newmexicostateparks.reserveamerica.com

It's best to resist the temptation to feed even the smallest wildlife.

US Army Corps of Engineers. Two campgrounds are managed by the US Army Corps of Engineers in New Mexico. As throughout the United States, New Mexico USACE parks offer excellence in campground design and maintenance. Drinking water, showers, and some electrical hookups are among the amenities. Operations are manned by paid camp hosts who are generally knowledgeable about the facility and surrounding area.

Fees are similar to state park fees. Reservations are available through www .recreation.gov.

US Army Corps of Engineers
Albuquerque District
4101 Jefferson Plaza NE
Albuquerque, NM 87109-3435
(505) 342-3349
www.spa.usace.army.mil/

National Forests. New Mexico has five national forests, encompassing almost 10 million acres. All offer campgrounds with similar facilities. Look for picnic tables, fire rings with grills, vault toilets, and, in some cases, drinking water.

Many Forest Service campgrounds are scheduled for improvements to make sites more accessible and amenities more modern. Some of these changes are designed to reduce human impact on the forest. This often means fewer and smaller campgrounds with sites spaced closer together and accessible by paved roads.

While these changes will make the campgrounds more appealing to some, others may want to look into less-structured camping choices. The changes also affect dispersed camping, which is no longer allowed in some national forest areas. It is wise to check with rangers before embarking on any camping trip into a national forest.

For more information:
Carson National Forest
208 Cruz Alta Rd.
Taos, NM 87571
(505) 758-6200

Developed campgrounds are an abundant feature in New Mexico.
COURTESY OF US BUREAU OF LAND MANAGEMENT

Dispersed camping is a common choice among tent campers in many areas of the state.

Cibola National Forest
2113 Osuna Rd. NE, Ste. A
Albuquerque, NM 87113-1001
(505) 346-3900

Gila National Forest
3005 E. Camino del Bosque
Silver City, NM 88061
(505) 388-8201

Lincoln National Forest
3463 Las Palomas
Alamogordo, NM 88310
(505) 434-7200

Santa Fe National Forest
11 Forest Ln.
Santa Fe, NM 87505
(505) 438-5300

National Parks. There are ten national monuments, two national historical parks, and one national park in New Mexico. Organized camping operated by the National Park Service is available at only three of these parks: Bandelier National Monument, Chaco Culture National Historical Park, and El Morro National Monument.

National Park Service campgrounds are typically sparse in amenities, with the focus being on the quality of the park rather than on the comfort of the visitor. Expect small campgrounds, tight spacing, picnic tables, and restrooms.

Having said that, keep in mind that these parks offer something you won't find anywhere else—educational opportunities ranging from archeological to geological. The campgrounds are usually designed for minimal impact on the area, so don't come here looking for luxury or extra amenities. Fees at the national parks are slightly higher than at Forest Service camps, but they remain a travel bargain. All sites operate on a first-come, first-served basis.

For more information:

National Parks Service
Intermountain Region
12795 Alameda Pkwy.
Denver, CO 80225
(303) 969-2500
www.nps.gov/state/nm

Bureau of Land Management. The Bureau of Land Management is the single largest landholder in the state of New Mexico. And while recreation isn't its top priority, plenty of opportunities exist. Development at Bureau of Land Management recreation sites varies widely. In general, expect only picnic tables and toilets and campgrounds that are sometimes indistinguishable from Forest Service camps.

Fees at Bureau of Land Management campgrounds mirror Forest Service fees. Many locations are free; others charge a fee that ranges between $5 and $10. No reservations are taken for these recreation areas.

For more information:
Bureau of Land Management
New Mexico State Office
301 Dinosaur Trail
PO Box 27115
Santa Fe, NM 87502-0115
(505) 954-2000
www.blm.gov/nm

New Mexico Game and Fish Department. The camping areas managed by the Game and Fish Department are by far the most primitive in the state. Expect little more than dispersed camping on the shores of a lake, with toilet facilities provided. The good news is that these areas offer some of the best lake fishing in the state at little or no cost. Crowds are usually not a problem either.

For more information:
New Mexico Department of Game and Fish
PO Box 25112
Santa Fe, NM 87504
(505) 827-7911
www.wildlife.state.nm.us

Camping Etiquette

Camping rule number one is this: Remember that you are not at home, and you're usually not alone. Rule number two is this: Follow all posted rules. These rules may seem arbitrary to you, but be assured that they serve a purpose. Beyond these two, the following are a few general camping guidelines that can help make the entire camping experience more pleasant for all of us.

- **Don't offend other people's senses.** Consider the impact of everything you do on fellow campers. Every noise you make, every flashlight you shine, and every smelly pile your dog leaves behind is an interruption of someone else's pleasure.
- **Share space graciously.** The close quarters of some campgrounds force us to share everything from plumbing to parking. The best measure is to never

use more than your neighbor does. Don't take up an extra parking space. Don't spread your camp to the limits. Don't hog the water or the water faucet. Nobody wants to see your dish towels or bath soap at the community water faucet.

- **Leave your campsite better than you found it.** Always do more than just clean up after yourself. Take a minute to pick up the trash left behind by the guy before you. Close all garbage cans and restroom doors.

- **Learn how to camp lightly.** This means having the least possible impact on the environment. If we are going to be allowed to continue camping in national forests and state parks, those of us who are vehicle campers would be wise to study the practices that have become standard for backcountry campers.

These rules are not designed to limit your fun, but rather to enhance everyone's long-term enjoyment of our natural resources.

Map Legend

Transportation

═⟨95⟩═ Interstate Highway

═⟨1⟩═ US Highway

═⟨161⟩═ State Highway

═⟨33⟩═ Forest/County Road

════ Local Road

Land Management

National Park/Forest

Wilderness Area/Indian Reservation

Symbols

① Campground

✪ Capital

○ City/Town

■ Point of Interest

Water Features

Body of Water

River/Creek

Northwest

If you are looking for a place away from the crowds where you can steep yourself in the magic of a less-developed New Mexico, this is the region for you. Here you can enjoy lush, green mountains or red rock deserts, calm lakes or rushing rivers. Spend your days exploring ancient ruins or soaking away your cares in hot mineral springs. Campgrounds are numerous, but people and civilization are in somewhat short supply, so plan your trip to the northwest accordingly.

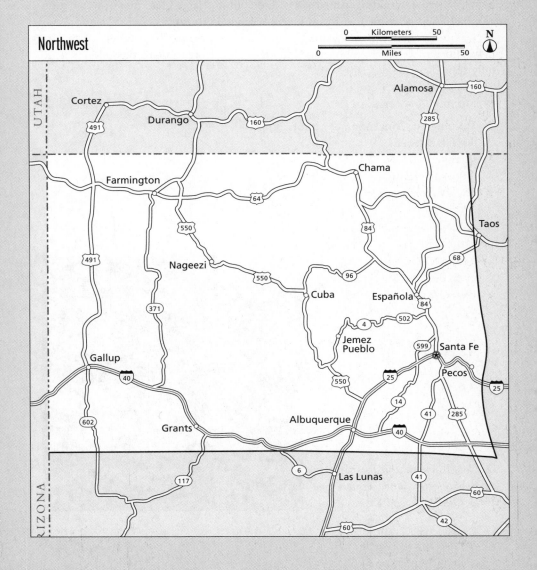

Farmington

Welcome to the badlands. The northwest corner of New Mexico, the area surrounding Farmington, is harsh, rugged, and has remained mostly undisturbed for centuries. It has been home for many cultures, but never densely populated. The major landholder in the area is the Navajo Nation, followed by the Bureau of Land Management.

The city of Farmington presents a delightful venture into an authentic Southwest lifestyle that has resisted the glitz of many larger southwestern cities. Galleries, museums, and restaurants entice you to step in from the heat and slow your pace.

Heat is a critical factor in planning your camping trip to the Farmington area. High temperatures in excess of 90 degrees F throughout the summer months, combined with low humidity, create the need to consume large quantities of water, most of which must be hauled with you when camping in the area.

Camping choices near Farmington include sites on the blue waters of Navajo Lake and remote campgrounds at Angel Peak and Buzzard Park that allow you to fully appreciate the desert beauty.

For more information:

Farmington Convention & Visitors Bureau
3041 E. Main St.
Farmington, NM 87402
(800) 448-1240
www.farmingtonnm.org

Aztec Chamber of Commerce
110 N. Ash
Aztec, NM 87410
(505) 334-7646
www.aztecchamber.com

Developed campsites in the northeast corner of the state attract visitors from Texas, Oklahoma, and Kansas.

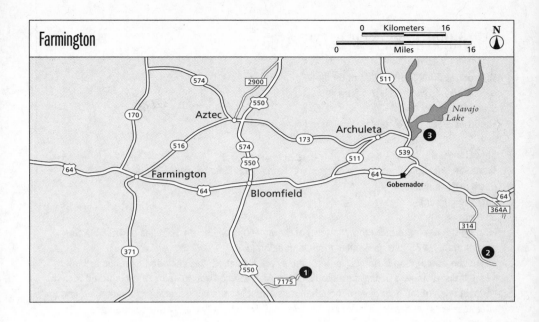

Farmington

		Group sites	RV sites	Total # of sites	Max. RV length	Hookups	Toilets	Showers	Drinking water	Dump station	Pets	Wheelchair	Recreation	Fee	Season	Can reserve	Stay limit
1	Angel Peak	·		9			V			·			H	$			14
2	Buzzard Park			4			V			·			HOR	$	May–Nov		14
3	Navajo Lake State Park	·	·	244		WES	F	·	·	·	·	·	HSFBL	$-$$			14

Hookups: W = Water, E = Electric, S = Sewer

Toilets: F = Flush, V = Vault, P = Pit, C = Chemical

Recreation: H = Hiking, S = Swimming, F = Fishing, B = Boating, L = Boat Launch, O = Off-Highway Driving,
  R = Horseback Riding

Fee (per-night campsite cost): $ = $0 to $5; $$ = $6 to $10; $$$ = $11 to $20.

Maximum Trailer/RV length given in feet. Stay limit given in days. If no entry under Maximum RV length where RV sites are
  available, no restriction is in place.

If no entry under Season, campground is open all year. If no entry under Fee, camping is free.

1 Angel Peak Recreation Area

Location: 20 miles southeast of Bloomfield
GPS: N36 31.337' / W107 55.947'
Sites: 9 sites for tents
Facilities: Vault toilets, tables, grills, and hiking trails
Fee: $
Elevation: 6,650 feet
Management: Bureau of Land Management, Farmington Field Office; (505) 564-7600
Reservations: None
Activities: Hiking
Season: Year-round
Finding the campground: From the town of Bloomfield, travel south 15 miles on US 550. Turn east onto CR 7175 and go 6 miles to the campground.
About the campground: Named for a towering rock formation, this secluded campground offers hiking trails, dispersed hiking, and scenic overlooks that allow you to enjoy the sculptured rocks and rich hues of the high desert. Though understandably sparse in vegetation, the campground is adequate for a getaway or a stopover. The area has been heavily explored for oil and gas. Unfortunately, this has left pump sites and drilling pads to mar what was previously pristine scenery. The campground and picnic areas do attract some locals, but otherwise it's quiet. This is a pack-it-in, pack-it-out camp, and no water is available.

2 Buzzard Park

Location: 31 miles southwest of Dulce
GPS: N36 52.871' / W107 13.0052'
Sites: 4 sites for tents
Facilities: Vault toilets, tables, and grills
Fee: $
Elevation: 7,300 feet
Management: Carson National Forest, Jicarilla Ranger District; (505) 632-2956
Reservations: None
Activities: Hiking and four-wheel driving
Season: May through November
Finding the campground: From Dulce travel 18 miles southwest on US 64. Turn north onto FR 310. Go 13 miles to the campground.
About the campground: Even the name of this campground is lonely. If solitude is your camping objective, this is a great place to leave the crowds behind. Opportunities for hiking and off-road driving are abundant and limited only by your vehicle and your willingness to leave this lovely campground.

3 Navajo Lake State Park

Location: 38 miles east of Farmington
GPS: N36 48.067' / W107 41.550'
Sites: 244 sites for tents and RVs
Facilities: Visitor center, group shelter, dump station, flush toilets, showers, marinas, playground, boat launch, and hiking trails; wheelchair-accessible facilities
Fee: $ to $$, annual permit available
Elevation: 6,100 feet
Management: New Mexico State Parks Department; (505) 632-2278; www.emnrd.state.nm.us/ SPD/navajolakestatepark.html
Reservations: None
Activities: Hiking, fishing, hunting, water sports, wildlife viewing, and scuba diving. Boat rentals are available at the marinas.
Season: Year-round
Finding the campground: From Farmington travel east 34 miles on US 64. Turn north onto NM 539. Go 4 miles to the main entrance.
About the campground: Navajo Lake is New Mexico's second-largest reservoir, with more than 15,000 surface acres when full. Fishing is possible for a full range of cold and warm water species, including trout and kokanee salmon. There are seven campgrounds, two marinas, paved trails, raised fishing platforms, and plenty of space to enjoy the outdoors. As with many of New Mexico's lakes, drought has caused lower-than-normal water levels at Navajo. Even at the lower levels, boating, fishing, and water activities are possible.

Chama

The most striking thing about the area surrounding Chama is its diversity. As you travel north through Abiquiu, the orange and red canyon walls gradually give way to piñon-dotted mesas before you reach the tall pines that grace the weathered mountains around Chama.

A list of things to do in the region includes a scenic train ride on the Cumbres & Toltec Railroad, rock collecting near Abiquiu Dam, and a visit to the Tierra Wools Showroom in Los Ojos, or you can simply enjoy the natural beauty. Wildflowers are abundant in the spring, and wildlife throughout the year.

There are plenty of camping choices that allow you to fully enjoy the region. The Jicarilla Apache Indian Reservation offers camping at several lakes. Fishing here is outstanding but strictly regulated. It is advisable to obtain a complete set of these regulations before you pack for your trip.

Camping in the Carson and Santa Fe National Forests is possible at several designated campgrounds. These range in size from 4 sites to 52 and offer typical Forest Service amenities. Two state parks also provide camping and fishing opportunities: El Vado and Heron Lakes are located in the Rio Chama State Recreation

Area. You'll find the campgrounds at these two sites a step up from the national forest camps.

Abiquiu Lake is one of the two US Army Corps of Engineers recreation facilities in New Mexico. If you've never camped at a USACE campground, consider giving it a try here at Abiquiu. The campgrounds are full-service and well designed.

For more information:
Chama Valley Chamber of Commerce
PO Box 306-RB
Chama, NM 87520
(800) 477-0149
www.chamavalley.com

Jicarilla Apache Indian Reservation, Fish & Game Department
PO Box 313
Dulce, NM 87528
(575) 759-3255
www.jicarillahunt.com

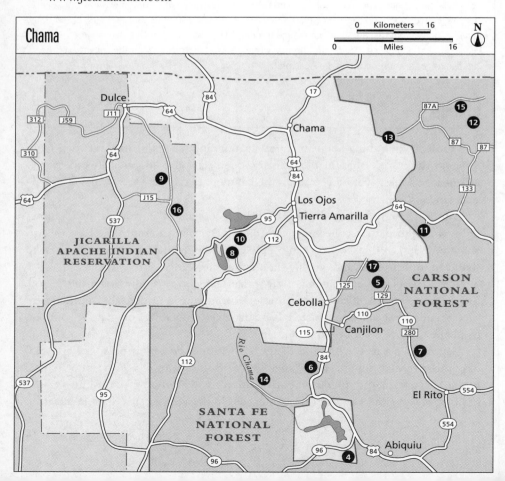

		Group sites	RV sites	Total # of sites	Max. RV length	Hookups	Toilets	Showers	Drinking water	Dump station	Pets	Wheelchair	Recreation	Fee	Season	Can reserve	Stay limit
4	Abiquiu Lake	·	·	54			FV	·	·	·	·	·	HSFB	$$		·	14
5	Canjilon Lakes		·	52			V		·		·		HF	$	May–Sept		14
6	Echo Amphitheater	·	·	10			V		·		·		H	$$			
7	El Rito Creek		·	11	22		V				·		FO	$	Apr–Nov		14
8	El Vado Lake State Park		·	80		E	F	·	·	·	·		SF	$$$	Apr–Nov		14
9	Enbom Lake	·		D			V				·		FB	$			
10	Heron Lake	·	·	254		WE	F	·	·	·	·	·	HSFBL	$$$			14
11	Hopewell Lake State Wildlife Area			34			V				·		FBHR	$$$	May–Oct	·	14
12	Laguna Larga			4			V						FB	$	May–Oct		
13	Lagunitas			20			V						FR	$	May–Oct		14
14	Rio Chama			11	16		V						FHS	$	Apr–Oct		14
15	Rio de los Pinos			4			V				·		F	$	May–Sept		14
16	Stone Lake		·	24		WES	V				·		FB	$			
17	Trout Lakes			12			V				·		F	$	May–Sept		14

Hookups: W = Water,   E = Electric,   S = Sewer

Toilets: F = Flush,   V = Vault,   P = Pit,   C = Chemical

Recreation: H = Hiking,   S = Swimming,   F = Fishing,   B = Boating,   L = Boat Launch,   O = Off-Highway Driving,   R = Horseback Riding

Fee (per-night campsite cost): $ = $0 to $5; $$ = $6 to $10; $$$ = $11 to $20.

Maximum Trailer/RV length given in feet. Stay limit given in days. If no entry under Maximum RV length where RV sites are available, no restriction is in place.

If no entry under Season, campground is open all year. If no entry under Fee, camping is free.

Snow-capped peaks create spring runoff, filling streams and ponds in the northwest region.

4 Abiquiu Lake (Riana Campground)

Location: 7 miles northwest of Abiquiu
GPS: N36 14.418' / W106 25379'
Sites: 54 sites for tents and RVs
Facilities: Flush and vault toilets, tables, grills, showers, drinking water, dump station, wheelchair-accessible sites, group sites, playground, and amphitheater
Fee: $$
Elevation: 6,283 feet
Management: US Army Corps of Engineers; (505) 685-4371
Reservations: www.recreation.gov
Activities: Hiking, swimming, fishing, boating, and rock collecting

Season: Year-round

Finding the campground: From the town of Abiquiu, travel 6 miles north on US 84. Turn west onto NM 96. Go about 1 mile to the campground.

About the campground: Abiquiu Lake represents the great possibilities that can be created when humans cooperate with nature. As part of the development plan for the watershed of the Rio Grande, the dam was completed in 1963. Rather than detract from the fragile natural surroundings, the clear water now mirrors them. The contrast between the red-and-gold, carved mesas and the blue water is a work of art. Cold-water fish such as trout, walleye, and kokanee salmon are caught regularly. A current fishing report is available online at www.wildlife.state.nm.us//fishing.

The Riana Campground offers comfort spiced with the desert scenery of the area. Spacing is acceptable, and the facilities are well maintained.

5 Canjilon Lakes

Location: 38 miles southeast of Chama
GPS: N36 32.999' / W106 20.617'
Sites: 52 sites for tents and RVs
Facilities: Vault toilets, drinking water, tables, and fire pits; wheelchair-accessible facilities
Fee: $
Elevation: 9,900 feet
Management: Carson National Forest, Canjilon Ranger District; (575) 684-2489
Reservations: None
Activities: Hiking and fishing
Season: May through September
Finding the campground: From Chama travel south 29 miles on US 84. Turn east onto NM 115 and go 2.5 miles to CR 280. Turn northeast and go 7.5 miles to FR 129. Turn north and go 1 mile to the campground.

About the campground: This popular string of campgrounds is testament to man's desire to catch fish even if the road into the area isn't so great. Though not as bad now as it was in years past, the road can still get rough after spring runoff. The three campgrounds (Upper, Middle, and Lower) are scattered among the piñon and provide plenty of room to spread out. Sites are well spaced, and this is one of only a few camps in the region with drinking water.

6 Echo Amphitheater

Location: 9 miles southwest of Canjilon
GPS: N36 21.504' / W106 31.505'
Sites: 10 sites for tents and RVs
Facilities: Vault toilets, tables, drinking water, and grills
Fee: $$
Elevation: 6,600 feet
Management: Carson National Forest, Canjilon Ranger District; (575) 684-2489

Reservations: None
Activities: Hiking
Season: Year-round
Finding the campground: From Canjilon travel 9.4 miles south on US 84. The campground and picnic area are on the west side of the highway.
About the campground: This campground makes an easy stopover on your way farther north or south on US 84. There is a short but interesting nature trail through the rock formations to the naturally formed amphitheater.

7 El Rito Creek

Location: 8 miles northwest of El Rito
GPS: N36 24.031' / W106 15.178'
Sites: 11 sites for tents and RVs
Facilities: Vault toilets, tables, and grills
Fee: $
Elevation: 7,600 feet
Management: Carson National Forest, El Rito Ranger Station; (575) 581-4554
Reservations: None
Activities: Fishing and four-wheel driving
Season: April through November
Finding the campground: From the town of El Rito on NM 554, travel north on NM 110 (which becomes CR 280) for about 8 miles to the campground.
About the campground: The soul of camping in this region rests in small camps like this one that are devoid of crowds, full of pine trees, and provide a decent place to fish. When the fish aren't biting, you'll want to break out the Forest Service maps for a bit of exploration along the myriad winding roads that crisscross these mountains. If you aren't the adventurous sort, just bring along a hammock, because this is a great place to hang it.

8 El Vado Lake State Park

Location: 13 miles southwest of Tierra Amarilla
GPS: N36 37.138' W106 44.146'
Sites: 80 sites for tents and RVs
Facilities: Flush toilets, drinking water, grills, tables, visitor center, electric sites, dump station, showers, trails, marina, and playground
Fee: $$$, annual permit available
Elevation: 6,900 feet
Management: New Mexico State Parks Department; (575) 588-7247; www.emnrd.state.nm.us/SPD/elvadolakestatepark.html
Reservations: None
Activities: Hiking and fishing

Season: April through November

Finding the campground: From Tierra Amarilla travel west on NM 532 for 1.5 miles. Turn south onto NM 112 and go 11 miles to the park road. Turn north and go 3.75 miles to the park entrance.

About the campground: Like many of New Mexico's state parks, El Vado presents you with an array of recreation choices set against a backdrop that showcases the best the state has to offer. This park offers fishing, winter cross-country skiing, and superb wildlife-watching opportunities. A 5.5-mile trail connects the park with nearby Heron Lake and is well worth the hike. Facilities at the campgrounds are typical of other state parks, well spaced, well planned, and well maintained.

9 Enbom Lake

Location: 11 miles southeast of Dulce
GPS: N36 47.639' / W106 52.834'
Sites: Dispersed
Facilities: Vault toilets, tables, and grills
Fee: $
Elevation: 7,864 feet
Management: Jicarilla Apache Reservation; (575) 759-3255
Reservations: None
Activities: Fishing and boating
Season: Year-round

Finding the campground: From Dulce travel south on Jicarilla Reservation Road J-8 about 11 miles to the lake.

About the campground: Another of the crown jewels of the Jicarilla Apache Reservation, Enbom languishes in the pines near the Continental Divide. Though the facilities are sparse, fishing is typically good and the scenery hard to beat.

10 Heron Lake State Park

Location: 9 miles west of Los Ojos
GPS: N36 40.274' / W106 41.373'
Sites: 254 sites for tents and RVs
Facilities: Flush toilets, electric sites, dump station, tables, grills, visitor center, group shelter, marina, and trails; wheelchair-accessible facilities
Fee: $$$, annual permit available
Elevation: 7,200 feet
Management: New Mexico State Parks Department; (575) 588-7470; www.emnrd.state.nm.us/SPD/heronlakestatepark.html
Reservations: None
Activities: Fishing, hiking, boating, and other water sports

The well-stocked lakes in the state park system make catching that first "big one" easy.

Season: Year-round
Finding the campground: From the town of Los Ojos on US 84, travel west about 9 miles on NM 95 to the park.
About the campground: Pack your sailboard and your wet suit when you get ready for your vacation at Heron Lake. Only no-wake speeds are allowed on the lake, and the gentle breezes entice many a sailor onto the cool waters. The setting is quiet and 100 percent New Mexico.

11 Hopewell Lake State Wildlife Area

Location: 21 miles east of Tierra Amarilla
GPS: N36 42.268' / W106 14.135'
Sites: 34 sites for tents and trailers
Facilities: Vault toilets, tables, and grills
Fee: $$$
Elevation: 9,600 feet
Management: Carson National Forest, Tres Piedras Ranger Station; (575) 758-8678
Reservations: None
Activities: Fishing and boating
Season: May through October

Finding the campground: From the southern intersection of US 64 and US 84, just south of Tierra Amarilla, travel east on US 64 about 21 miles to the campground.

About the campground: This 14-acre, high-country lake is hard to get to but worth the trip, particularly if you want to get away from the world. The same 10,000-foot pass that makes US 64 impassable in winter makes Hopewell Lake an incredible camping spot in summer. Fishing is generally good for rainbow and brook trout. The campground was renovated in 1998 to include the trailer sites. Nonmotorized boating is allowed.

12 Laguna Larga

Location: 25 miles southwest of Antonito, CO
GPS: N36 53.053' / W106 06.486'
Sites: 4 sites for tents
Facilities: Vault toilets, tables, and grills
Fee: $
Elevation: 9,000 feet
Management: Carson National Forest, Tres Piedras Ranger Station; (575) 758-8678
Reservations: None
Activities: Fishing, canoeing, wildlife watching
Season: May through October
Finding the campground: From Antonito travel south on US 285 about 4 miles. Turn west onto FR 87 and go 1.5 miles to FR 78. Turn north onto FR 78A and go 1.5 miles to the campground.
About the campground: The solitude and scenery make traveling this far off the grid worthwhile. Dispersed camping is allowed around the lake. Bring your fishing gear as the lake is the perfect spot to try your luck. Trash must be packed out.

13 Lagunitas

Location: 25 miles southwest of Antonito, CO
GPS: N36 53.070' / W106 19.248'
Sites: 20 sites for tents
Facilities: Vault toilets, tables, and grills
Fee: $
Elevation: 10,400 feet
Management: Carson National Forest, Tres Piedras Ranger Station; (575) 758-8678
Reservations: None
Activities: Fishing and horseback riding
Season: May through October
Finding the campground: From Antonito travel south on US 285 about 4 miles. Turn west onto FR 87 and go 21 miles to the campground.
About the campground: If you can get here, you'll love it. The road is long and dusty when it's dry and slippery when it's wet. The mountain scenery is almost unmatched anywhere in the

state. Fishing for rainbow and brook trout can be outstanding in the series of lakes at the head of Lagunitas Creek, so bring a hook and a book and plan to stay a while to enjoy the peace and quiet.

14 Rio Chama

Location: 21 miles northwest of Abiquiu
GPS: N36 21.308' / W106 40.364'
Sites: 11 sites for tents
Facilities: Vault toilets, tables, and grills
Fee: $
Elevation: 6,400 feet
Management: Santa Fe National Forest, Coyote Ranger District; (575) 638-5526
Reservations: None
Activities: Hiking, whitewater rafting, floating, fishing, and swimming
Season: April through October
Finding the campground: From Abiquiu travel north on US 84 about 15 miles. Turn onto FR 151 and go about 12 miles to the campground.
About the campground: If you can get here, you are in for a treat. This campground is off the beaten path, but offers access to the Chama River Canyon Wilderness for rafting, kayaking, and swimming. The wildlife is spectacular, as are the hiking possibilities. The road is not usable when wet, so plan an alternate campground if rain is in the forecast.

15 Rio de los Pinos

Location: 14 miles southwest of Antonito, CO
GPS: N36 57.736' / W106 9.568
Sites: 4 sites for tents
Facilities: Vault toilets, tables, and grills
Fee: $
Elevation: 8,200 feet
Management: Carson National Forest, Tres Piedras Ranger Station; (575) 758-8678
Reservations: None
Activities: Fishing
Season: May through September
Finding the campground: In Antonito travel south on CR 12.5 7.25 miles until it merges with Los Pinos River Access Road/FR284/FR87A. Continue west for about 7 miles to the camping areas.
About the campground: Situated just outside the Los Pinos State Recreation Area, this campground has the river, it has the fish, and it has the mountains and pines. The only thing missing is you.

16 Stone Lake

Location: 17 miles southeast of Dulce
GPS: N36 43.392' / W106 53.147'
Sites: 24 sites for tents and RVs
Facilities: Vault toilets, tables, electricity, and grills
Fee: $
Elevation: 7,247 feet
Management: Jicarilla Game and Fish; (575) 759-3255; www.jicarillahunt.com/camping
Reservations: None
Activities: Fishing and boating
Season: Year-round
Finding the campground: From Dulce travel south 17 miles on Jicarilla Reservation Road J-8 to the lake.
About the campground: Stone Lake offers the most structured campground of all the Jicarilla Reservation lakes. Like the others, the setting is pleasant, the fish numerous, and the crowds relatively small. A valid Jicarilla fishing permit is required to camp.

17 Trout Lakes

Location: 8.5 miles northeast of Cebolla
GPS: N36 36.534' / W106 22.952'
Sites: 12 sites for tents
Facilities: Vault toilets, tables, and grills
Fee: $
Elevation: 9,300 feet
Management: Carson National Forest, Canjilon Ranger Station; (575) 684-2486
Reservations: None
Activities: Fishing and nonmotorized boating
Season: May through September
Finding the campground: From the town of Cebolla on US 84, travel northeast 8.5 miles on FR 125 to the campground.
About the campground: The name of this string of clear mountain lakes just about says all you need to know. The trout fishing is good, the scenery even better.

Cuba

The town of Cuba is the gateway to much of New Mexico's Indian culture to the west and the lush national forests to the east. The town itself is small but serves as the commercial center for the eastern edge of the Navajo Nation.

The name "Cuba" means large tank or vat. According to Indian legend, the area was once completely filled with water. Land formations to the west bear out that story in fossil-bearing layers of red silt and clay.

All roads east lead into the Santa Fe National Forest and to the edge of the San Pedro Parks Wilderness Area, where the fishing is world-class and the scenery idyllic.

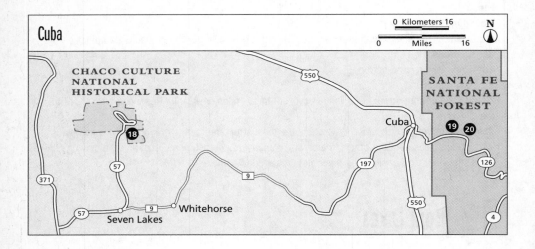

		Group sites	RV sites	Total # of sites	Max. RV length	Hookups	Toilets	Showers	Drinking water	Dump station	Pets	Wheelchair	Recreation	Fee	Season	Can reserve	Stay limit
18	Chaco Culture NHP	·	·	68	30		F		·	·	·	·	H	$$		·	7
19	Clear Creek		·	12	30		V		·		·	·	HF	$	May–Oct		14
20	Rio de las Vacas		·	15	16		V		·		·		HF	$	May–Oct		14

Hookups: W = Water,   E = Electric,   S = Sewer
Toilets: F = Flush,   V = Vault,   P = Pit,   C = Chemical
Recreation: H = Hiking,   S = Swimming,   F = Fishing,   B = Boating,   L = Boat Launch,   O = Off-Highway Driving,
    R = Horseback Riding
Fee (per-night campsite cost): $ = $0 to $5; $$ = $6 to $10; $$$ = $11 to $20.
Maximum Trailer/RV length given in feet. Stay limit given in days. If no entry under Maximum RV length where RV sites are
    available, no restriction is in place.
If no entry under Season, campground is open all year. If no entry under Fee, camping is free.

18 Chaco Culture National Historical Park

Location: 87 miles west of Cuba
GPS: N36 03.684' / W107 57.730'
Sites: 68 sites for tents and RVs
Facilities: Flush toilets, dump station, visitor center, group sites, and wheelchair-accessible sites
Fee: $$
Elevation: 6,300 feet
Management: National Park Service; (505) 786-7061; www.nps.gov/chcu/
Reservations: www.recreation.gov
Activities: Hiking, exploring historical ruins, and biking
Season: Year-round
Finding the campground: From Cuba travel west on NM 197 (which becomes N-9) about 67 miles to Seven Lakes. Turn north onto N-14, following the signs 20 miles to the park.
About the campground: This premier archeological park is breathtaking in its historical beauty. The multistory dwellings found here present an unrivaled example of Pueblo pre-Columbian civilization. Come here looking for the history, not for the facilities. The last 20 miles of road are dirt; let that be a signal to the level of amenities at the park. Sites have tables and fire rings, but not much else. Drinking water is available only at the visitor center, so it's best to bring your own. You must also bring your own firewood or charcoal; none is available at the campground.

In addition to the eight self-guided trails through the ruins, hikers will find four backcountry trails to more remote areas of the canyon. There are also designated bicycle trails. As a word of caution, this is harsh terrain, with an even harsher climate. To fully enjoy your visit to Chaco, plan and pack wisely.

19 Clear Creek

Location: 12 miles east of Cuba
GPS: N35 59.801' / W106 49.586'
Sites: 12 sites for tents and RVs
Facilities: Vault toilets, drinking water, tables, and grills; wheelchair-accessible facilities
Fee: $
Elevation: 8,500 feet
Management: Santa Fe National Forest, Cuba Ranger District; (505) 289-3264
Activities: Hiking and fishing
Season: May through October
Finding the campground: From Cuba travel east on NM 126 (which becomes FR 126) about 12 miles to the campground.
About the campground: The western edge of the Santa Fe National Forest is "the road less traveled" that you've been longing for. The once busy mining and logging roads are now rutted and all but abandoned. Of course, that means heaven to four-wheel drive enthusiasts. Using Forest Service maps, you could explore for days and not run out of roads. Rockhounds will thrill at narrow tracks littered with malachite slivers. Wildlife watchers can set their scopes on black bear and deer

that have had little exposure to humans. The campground is small, but pine-shaded sites offer a bit of space between campers.

20 Rio de las Vacas

Location: 13 miles east of Cuba
GPS: N35 59.802' / W106 48.367'
Sites: 15 sites for tents and RVs
Facilities: Vault toilets, drinking water, tables, and grills
Fee: $
Elevation: 8,500 feet
Management: Santa Fe National Forest, Cuba Ranger District; (505) 289-3264
Activities: Hiking and fishing
Season: May through October
Finding the campground: From Cuba travel east on NM 126 (which becomes FR 126) about 13 miles to the campground.
About the campground: Like its neighbor (Clear Creek), Rio de las Vacas offers the outdoor adventurer a retreat from the crowded eastern half of the state and a look at New Mexico's national forests as they were several decades ago. The added bonus here is access to Rio de las Vacas, which offers decent trout fishing.

Jemez Springs

If you don't know the Jemez Springs area, it's no surprise, because not a lot of people do. Finding it is like discovering the place where the locals hang out just around the bend from the high-profile places to which the tourists flock. As you enter Jemez country, you pass through the Jemez Pueblo Reservation. The red canyon walls set the stage for your journey into the magical valley. You can't really experience Jemez until you've had Indian fry bread dripping with honey, so go ahead and stop at the roadside stands.

The bread is just the beginning of what could lead to sensory overload if your visit to Jemez is too rushed. Slow down and enjoy the sights and the people. Stop at Soda Dam, a naturally formed mineral dam that resembles cave formations usually found deep in the earth. Hike to Jemez Falls (there's a long trail and a short one). Visit the hot springs (if you're the adventurous sort) or one of the state's premier wineries in Ponderosa. Tour the Seven Springs Fish Hatchery. Eat a green chile burger in La Cueva. Take a relaxing mineral bath and massage at the local bathhouse. Want more to do? How about a scenic drive to the Gilman Tunnels? Or perhaps an afternoon collecting Apache tears (small pebbles of obsidian)? There's always an educational visit to Bandelier National Monument. Still not enough? You could cast a line in the Jemez River and while away the hours hauling in the trout.

Scenic driving is a favorite activity in this area of the state.

For more information:
Village of Jemez Springs
www.jemezsprings.org

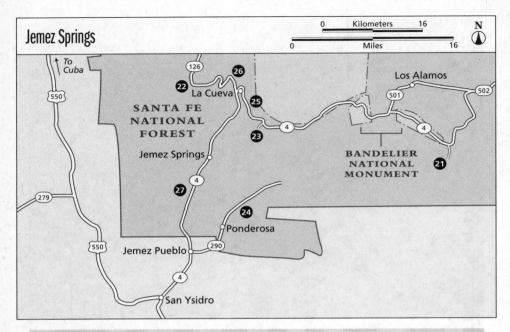

		Group sites	RV sites	Total # of sites	Max. RV length	Hookups	Toilets	Showers	Drinking water	Dump station	Pets	Wheelchair	Recreation	Fee	Season	Can reserve	Stay limit
21	**Bandelier NM**	·	·	94			F		·	·	·	·	HFR	$$	Apr–Oct		7
22	**Fenton Lake SP**	·	·	40		WE	V		·		·	·	HFB	$–$$	Apr–Oct	·	14
23	**Jemez Falls**		·	52	22		V		·		·		HF	$$			14
24	**Paliza**	·	·	23	16		V		·		·		HO	$$		·	14
25	**Redondo**		·	59	45		V		·		·		H	$$			14
26	**San Antonio**		·	29	35		V		·		·		HF	$$		·	14
27	**Vista Linda**		·	13	40	W	V		·		·		HF	$$			14

Hookups: W = Water,   E = Electric,   S = Sewer

Toilets: F = Flush,   V = Vault,   P = Pit,   C = Chemical

Recreation: H = Hiking,   S = Swimming,   F = Fishing,   B = Boating,   L = Boat Launch,   O = Off-Highway Driving,
   R = Horseback Riding

Fee (per-night campsite cost): $ = $0 to $5; $$ = $6 to $10; $$$ = $11 to $20.

Maximum Trailer/RV length given in feet. Stay limit given in days. If no entry under Maximum RV length where RV sites are
   available, no restriction is in place.

If no entry under Season, campground is open all year. If no entry under Fee, camping is free.

21 Bandelier National Monument

Location: 10 miles southeast of Los Alamos
GPS: N35 46.730' / W106 16.250'
Sites: 94 sites for tents and RVs
Facilities: Flush toilets, drinking water, tables, grills, group sites, wheelchair-accessible sites, and dump station
Fee: $$
Elevation: 6,700 feet
Management: National Park Service; (505) 672-3861, ext. 517; www.nps.gov/band/
Reservations: None
Activities: Hiking, fishing, horseback riding, and exploring historical sites
Season: April through October
Finding the campground: From Los Alamos travel about 5 miles south on NM 501. Turn east onto NM 4 and go about 5 miles to the park entrance.
About the campground: The opportunity to visit thirteenth-century Pueblo Indian cliff dwellings doesn't come along every day. If you're in the Jemez area, it's worth the drive to this monument.

The campground itself is nothing out of the ordinary. Typical of the National Park Service, emphasis is on experiencing the location with as little disruption of natural surroundings as possible. For the adventurous, however, there are over 70 miles of hiking trails that provide additional camping opportunities in the backcountry of the monument. If you are willing to forgo the comforts of vehicle camping, this is the best way to truly enjoy the sights that Bandelier has to offer.

22 Fenton Lake State Park

Location: 13 miles northwest of Jemez Springs
GPS: N35 53.001' / W106 43.357'
Sites: 40 sites for tents and RVs
Facilities: Vault toilets, drinking water, tables, grills, group sites, wheelchair-accessible sites, electricity, and playground
Fee: $ to $$, annual permit available
Elevation: 7,900 feet
Management: New Mexico State Parks Department; (575) 829-3630; www.emnrd.state.nm.us/SPD/fentonlakestatepark.html
Reservations: Call (877) 664-7787; http://newmexicostateparks.reserveamerica.com
Activities: Hiking, fishing, and boating; snowmobiling, cross-country skiing, and ice fishing in winter
Season: April through October
Finding the campground: From Jemez Springs travel north on NM 4 about 8 miles to the village of La Cueva. Turn west onto NM 126 (which becomes FR 126) and go about 5 miles to the park entrance.
About the campground: If you have plans to see the sights and enjoy the activities in the Jemez area, it will be difficult to do from here. The problem isn't access, but rather lack of willingness to leave once you get here. The lake and surrounding scenery create an idyllic location for doing a whole lot of nothing. The fishing is good, especially if you bring a canoe. If the fish aren't biting, the combination of ponderosa pines and prolific wildflowers provides the perfect place to nap.

The campground is laid out much like a national forest camp, with the bonus of some sites with electric hookups. With 40 sites to choose from, almost all with views of the lake, there's bound to be one to your liking.

23 Jemez Falls

Location: 15 miles northeast of Jemez Springs
GPS: N35 49.445' / W106 36.353'
Sites: 52 sites for tents and RVs
Facilities: Vault toilets, drinking water, tables, grills, group sites, and wheelchair-accessible sites
Fee: $$
Elevation: 7,900 feet
Management: Santa Fe National Forest, Jemez Ranger District; (575) 829-3535
Reservations: None
Activities: Hiking and fishing
Season: Year-round
Finding the campground: From Jemez Springs travel 15 miles north and then east on NM 4 to Jemez Falls Road. Turn south and go 0.75 miles to the campground.
About the campground: The sites at this camp are well spaced among the pines, with the added attraction of a short trail leading to the falls. Trail 137 is a wonderful hike (1.5 miles) that takes you back across the mountain to the east, ending at Battleship Rock. Overall, the camp is a near-perfect spot from which to enjoy everything the Jemez Valley has to offer.

24 Paliza

Location: 7.5 miles northeast of Jemez Pueblo
GPS: N35 41.835' / W106 38.05'
Sites: 23 sites for tents and RVs, plus dispersed camping and group sites
Facilities: Vault toilets, drinking water, tables, grills, and group sites
Fee: $$
Elevation: 5,800 feet
Management: Santa Fe National Forest, Jemez Ranger District; (575) 829-3535
Reservations: Call (877) 444-6777; www.reserveamerica.com
Activities: Hiking, four-wheel driving, rock collecting, and wildlife viewing
Season: Year-round
Finding the campground: At Jemez Pueblo (not Jemez Springs), turn east onto NM 290 (which becomes FR 266) and go 7.5 miles to the campground.
About the campground: Don't care about fishing? Just looking for a place to escape the crowds? Paliza is calling your name. This is the only camp in the western Santa Fe National Forest that offers three-sided Adirondack shelters with stone fireplaces. There are only three available, so reservations are highly recommended. There is room for small and medium-sized trailers to park next to the shelters. There are also tent sites scattered across the hillside.

Adirondack shelters like this one at Paliza are a treat at some campgrounds in the Santa Fe National Forest.

Bring your binoculars because the wildlife at this isolated camp is abundant. Daytime hours treat you to huge numbers of hummingbirds, while dusk signals the graceful airborne dance of bats that live in nearby cliffside caves.

25 Redondo

Location: 11 miles northeast of Jemez Springs
GPS: N35 51.801' / W106 37.569'
Sites: 59 sites for tents and RVs
Facilities: Vault toilets, drinking water, tables, and grills
Fee: $$
Elevation: 8,100 feet
Management: Santa Fe National Forest, Jemez Ranger District; (575) 829-3535
Reservations: None
Activities: Hiking and scenic driving
Season: Year-round
Finding the campground: From Jemez Springs travel 11 miles north and then east on NM 4 to the campground.

About the campground: Like the campground at Jemez falls, Redondo puts you in the middle of the action. Anything you'd want to do in the valley is a short drive away. The camp is large, but the sites are well spaced to provide some privacy.

26 San Antonio

Location: 9.5 miles north of Jemez Springs
GPS: N35 53.218' / W106 38.769'
Sites: 29 sites for tents and RVs
Facilities: Vault toilets, drinking water, tables, and grills
Fee: $$
Elevation: 6,800 feet
Management: Santa Fe National Forest, Jemez Ranger District; (575) 829-3535
Reservations: Call (877) 444-6777; www.reserveamerica.com
Activities: Hiking and fishing
Season: Year-round
Finding the campground: From Jemez Springs travel 7.5 miles north on NM 4 to the village of La Cueva. Turn west onto NM 126 and go 2 miles to the campground.
About the campground: Break out the hammock for this campground. It perches on the hillside among the pines and aspens and has a relaxing feel. It's still close enough to the action in the valley that you can fish, hike, or be a tourist easily (after your nap, that is.) Reservations are recommended.

27 Vista Linda

Location: 5 miles south of Jemez Springs
GPS: N35 42.985' / W106 43.319'
Sites: 13 sites for tents and RVs
Facilities: Vault toilets, drinking water, tables, and grills
Fee: $$
Elevation: 5,800 feet
Management: Santa Fe National Forest, Jemez Ranger District; (575) 829-3535
Reservations: None
Activities: Hiking and fishing
Season: Year-round
Finding the campground: From Jemez Springs travel south on NM 4 to the campground, located on the west side of the highway.
About the campground: This is the lowest-elevation campground in the Jemez Valley. Its easy access to the highway makes it perfect for RVs up to 40 feet long. This campground might be the most convenient spot from which to enjoy everything the valley has to offer.

Española-Santa Fe

If you're considering a camping vacation to this area, you've chosen the heart of New Mexico. It's all here: aspens and pines, mountains, food, art, and air so fresh you can almost taste it. The downside to traveling in and around Santa Fe is that you are not alone in your quest for a New Mexican adventure. Visitors flock here by the thousands, swelling the city to twice its normal size on summer weekends. Camping in the surrounding mountains is one way to lose part of the crowd, but rest assured, not all.

The best way to get away from fellow travelers is to venture onto forest roads and hiking trails, both of which are abundant in the area. Then after a long day's trek you can fully appreciate the joy of companionship and the flavors of Santa Fe.

For more information:
Santa Fe County Chamber of Commerce
1644 St. Michael's Dr.
Santa Fe, NM 87505
(505) 988-3279
www.santafechamber.com

Española Valley Chamber of Commerce
1 Calle de las Espanolas, Stes. F and G
PO Box 190
Española, NM 87532
(505) 753-2831
www.espanolanmchamber.com

La Cieneguilla Petroglyph Site is very close to the city of Santa Fe. COURTESY OF US BUREAU OF LAND MANAGEMENT

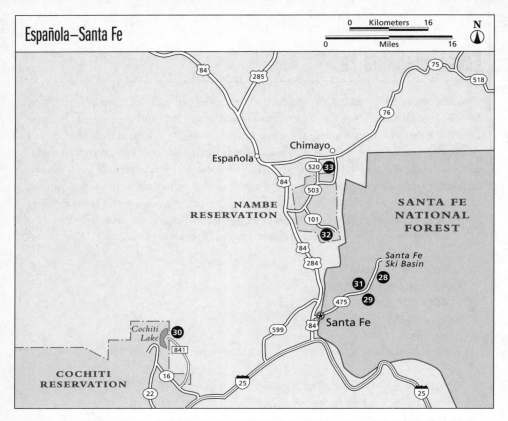

		Group sites	RV sites	Total # of sites	Max. RV length	Hookups	Toilets	Showers	Drinking water	Dump station	Pets	Wheelchair	Recreation	Fee	Season	Can reserve	Stay limit
28	**Big Tesuque**		·	7			V				·	·	HF	$$	May–Oct		14
29	**Black Canyon**		·	24			V		·		·		H	$$	May–Oct	·	14
30	**Cochiti Lake**		·	141		WE	F		·	·	·	·	HSFBL	$$			14
31	**Hyde Memorial SP**		·	50		E	V		·	·	·		H	$–$$			14
32	**Nambé Falls**		D		22	E	V		·				HF	$$$	Mar–Oct		14
33	**Santa Cruz Lake**		D				V		·		·	·	HSF	$$			14

Hookups: W = Water, E = Electric, S = Sewer

Toilets: F = Flush, V = Vault, P = Pit, C = Chemical

Recreation: H = Hiking, S = Swimming, F = Fishing, B = Boating, L = Boat Launch, O = Off-Highway Driving,
  R = Horseback Riding

Fee (per-night campsite cost): $ = $0 to $5; $$ = $6 to $10; $$$ = $11 to $20.

Maximum Trailer/RV length given in feet. Stay limit given in days. If no entry under Maximum RV length where RV sites are
  available, no restriction is in place.

If no entry under Season, campground is open all year. If no entry under Fee, camping is free.

28 Big Tesuque

Location: 11 miles northeast of Santa Fe
GPS: N35 46.152' / W105 48.551'
Sites: 7 sites for tents and RVs
Facilities: Vault toilets, grills, wheelchair-accessible sites, and tables
Fee: $$
Elevation: 9,700 feet
Management: Santa Fe National Forest; (505) 753-7331
Reservations: None
Activities: Hiking and fishing
Season: May through October
Finding the campground: In Santa Fe, from I-25 exit 282, travel north on US 285/84 for 3.6 miles to NM 475 (Hyde Park Road). Turn east, following the signs to the Santa Fe Ski Basin, and go about 11 miles to the campground.
About the campground: Big Tesuque (tess-su-kee) is one of a string of campgrounds on Hyde Park Road on the way to the Santa Fe Ski Basin. The pines and aspen reign over a land of winding streams, gentle waterfalls, and busy wildlife. Spend a day here and you begin to understand why artists flock to the area: The place itself is an inspiring work of art.

29 Black Canyon

Location: 7.5 miles northeast of Santa Fe
GPS: N35 43.672' / W105 50.388'
Sites: 24 sites for tents and RVs
Facilities: Vault toilets, grills, tables, wheelchair-accessible sites, and drinking water
Fee: $$
Elevation: 8,400 feet
Management: Santa Fe National Forest; (505) 753-7331
Reservations: Call (877) 444-6777; www.reserveamerica.com
Activities: Hiking
Season: May through October
Finding the campground: In Santa Fe, from I-25 exit 282, travel north on US 285/84 for 3.6 miles to NM 475 (Hyde Park Road). Turn east, following the signs to the Santa Fe Ski Basin, and go about 7.5 miles to the campground.
About the campground: Reservations at Black Canyon are strongly encouraged. During the busy summer months, it is virtually the only way to secure a spot at this lovely but crowded camp. It's a nice place to lay your head after a day wandering the Santa Fe National Forest or perhaps the Pecos Wilderness, which is easily accessible via trails nearby.

30 Cochiti Lake

Location: 30 miles west of Santa Fe
GPS: N35 38.536' / W106 19.965'
Sites: 141 sites for tents and RVs
Facilities: Flush and vault toilets, tables, fire rings, boat launch, showers, dump station, electricity, and drinking water
Fee: $$
Elevation: 5,232 feet
Management: US Army Corps of Engineers; (505) 465-0307; www.spa.usace.army.mil/Missions/CivilWorks/Recreation/CochitiLake.aspx
Reservations: None
Activities: Hiking, swimming, fishing, boating, and golf
Season: Year-round
Finding the campground: Follow I-25 south of Santa Fe and take exit 264. Turn north onto NM 16, then west onto NM 22, 11 miles. Go straight on Cochiti Highway about a mile to the recreation area entrance.
About the campground: The ashen mesas surrounding Cochiti balance the blue waters of this flood control lake, which was built in 1975. The water beckons New Mexicans seeking relief from the summer heat, so don't come here to get away from the crowds; come instead to join the fun.

The campground facilities are certainly adequate for those looking for desert mountain scenery and water activities. Most of the roads are paved, many of the campsites have shelters, and some even have electrical hookups. Typical of Corps of Engineers campgrounds, the design and layout provide spacious sites to handle the crowds. The nearby Cochiti Lake Golf Course is public and provides a pleasant way of passing the time if the fish aren't biting.

31 Hyde Memorial State Park

Location: 8.5 miles northeast of Santa Fe
GPS: N35 43.816' / W105 50.247'
Sites: 50 sites for tents and RVs
Facilities: Vault toilets, tables, grills, sites with electricity, visitor center, playground, and dump station
Fee: $ to $$, annual permit available
Elevation: 8,500 feet
Management: New Mexico State Parks Department; (505) 983-7175; www.emnrd.state.nm.us/SPD/hydememorialstatepark.html
Reservations: Call (877) 664-7787; http://newmexicostateparks.reserveamerica.com
Activities: Hiking, cross-country skiing, and snowmobiling
Season: Year-round
Finding the campground: From I-25 in Santa Fe, take exit 282 and travel north 3.6 miles on US 285/84 to NM 475 (Hyde Park Road). Turn east, following the signs to the Santa Fe Ski Basin, and go about 8.5 miles to the campground.

About the campground: The Sangre de Cristo Mountains beg you to stop and stay a while. The perfect balance of pine and aspen contrasts sharply with gray rock walls. The nice part is that it's hard to see and do it all. There's always a trail to save for next time, always another adventure waiting. Hyde Park makes a great place from which to begin your explorations. The sites are well spaced and some have electrical hookups; others have three-sided Adirondack shelters for that extra bit of comfort you crave.

32 Nambé Falls

Location: 16 miles southeast of Española
GPS: N35 51.586' / W105 55.846'
Sites: Dispersed
Facilities: Vault toilets, drinking water, tables, grills, and electricity
Fee: $$$
Elevation: 6,600 feet
Management: Nambe Pueblo; (505) 455-2036; http://nambefalls.fatcow.com/rates.html
Reservations: None
Activities: Hiking and fishing
Season: March through October
Finding the campground: From Española travel southeast 8.5 miles on US 285/84. Turn east onto NM 503 and go 2.5 miles to Reservation Road 101. Turn south and go 5.5 miles to the campground.
About the campground: The campground at this scenic lake is small but continually improving. Because it is a bit out of the way, it doesn't attract as many of the Santa Fe tourists as you'll find in other campgrounds in the region. Come here to relax and enjoy the quiet of the mountains.

33 Santa Cruz Lake

Location: 13 miles east of Española
GPS: N35 58.815' / W105 55.014'
Sites: Dispersed
Facilities: Vault toilets, grills, picnic tables, wheelchair-accessible sites, and drinking water
Fee: $$
Elevation: 6,400 feet
Management: Bureau of Land Management; (575) 758-8851; www.blm.gov/nm
Reservations: None
Activities: Hiking, swimming, and fishing
Season: Year-round
Finding the campground: From Española travel 10 miles east on NM 76. Turn south onto NM 503 and go 1 mile to Santa Cruz Lake Road. Turn southwest and continue 1.5 miles to the dispersed camping areas.

About the campground: With the Sangre de Cristo Mountains as a backdrop, Santa Cruz Lake provides a quiet, low-altitude retreat for fishing or perhaps sailboarding. The lake is designated as a no-wake area.

Gallup

The far western reaches of New Mexico present an interesting blend of dusty red rock formations and pine forests, Native American history, and modern technology. Come here looking for blue sky and you'll find it in abundance over stretches of undeveloped land.

For more information:
Gallup–McKinley County Chamber of Commerce
106 W. Historic Hwy. 66
Gallup, NM 87301
(505) 722-2228 or (800) 380-4989
www.thegallupchamber.com

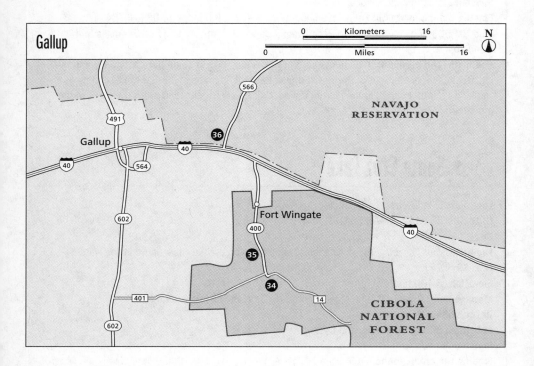

		Group sites	RV sites	Total # of sites	Max. RV length	Hookups	Toilets	Showers	Drinking water	Dump station	Pets	Wheelchair	Recreation	Fee	Season	Can reserve	Stay limit
34	McGaffey	•	•	49		E	V		•	•	•	•	HF	$$	May-Oct		14
35	Quaking Aspen		•	20	22		V		•		•		HF	$$	May-Oct		14
36	Red Rock Park		•	106		EW	F	•	•		•	•		$-$$			14

Hookups: W = Water,   E = Electric,   S = Sewer
Toilets: F = Flush,   V = Vault,   P = Pit,   C = Chemical
Recreation: H = Hiking,   S = Swimming,   F = Fishing,   B = Boating,   L = Boat Launch,   O = Off-Highway Driving,
   R = Horseback Riding
Fee (per-night campsite cost): $ = $0 to $5; $$ = $6 to $10; $$$ = $11 to $20.
Maximum Trailer/RV length given in feet. Stay limit given in days. If no entry under Maximum RV length where RV sites are
   available, no restriction is in place.
If no entry under Season, campground is open all year. If no entry under Fee, camping is free.

34 McGaffey

Location: 22 miles southeast of Gallup
GPS: N35 22.020' / W108 31.366'
Sites: 49 sites for tents and RVs
Facilities: Vault toilets, tables, grills, drinking water, electricity, and dump station; wheelchair-accessible facilities
Fee: $$
Elevation: 8,000 feet
Management: Cibola National Forest, Mt. Taylor Ranger District; (505) 287-8833, fee
Reservations: None
Activities: Hiking and fishing
Season: May through October
Finding the campground: From I-40 take exit 33 (11 miles east of Gallup) and travel southwest onto NM 400 for about 11 miles to the campground road. Turn south and go 0.5 mile to the campground.
About the campground: This is a very popular spot. The pines and scrub oaks offer a peaceful setting, the hiking is suitable for all skill levels, and the fishing is usually adequate for most anglers. McGaffey Lake is designated as no-wake.

McGaffey is one of the few national forest camps in the state with conveniences like electric hookups and an RV dump station, and like most campgrounds in popular areas, McGaffey fills to capacity during the height of the season.

35 Quaking Aspen

Location: 20 miles southeast of Gallup
GPS: N35 24.537' / W108 32.352'
Sites: 20 sites for tents and RVs
Facilities: Vault toilets, tables, grills, fishing, and drinking water
Fee: $$
Elevation: 7,600 feet
Management: Cibola National Forest, Mt. Taylor Ranger District; (505) 287-8833
Reservations: None
Activities: Hiking
Season: May through October
Finding the campground: From Gallup take I-40 east 11 miles to exit 33; then travel south on NM 400 for about 9 miles to the campground.
About the campground: Like its neighbor McGaffey, Quaking Aspen is popular due in part to the easy access to I-40. The scenery and fishing are additional drawing cards here. Either of these two camps makes a nice place to meet friends for a long weekend, but plan to arrive early to secure campsites.

36 Red Rock Park

Location: 9 miles east of Gallup
GPS: N35 32.292' / W108 36.346'
Sites: 106 sites for tents and RVs
Facilities: Flush toilets, tables, grills, drinking water, showers, and electricity
Fee: $ to $$
Elevation: 6,600 feet
Management: City of Gallup; (505) 722-3839; www.gallupnm.gov/index.aspx?NID=207
Reservations: None
Activities: Scenic driving, rodeos, and festivals
Season: Year-round
Finding the campground: From Gallup take I-40 east to exit 31 at Navajo Wingate Village. The park entrance is on the service road near the exit ramp.
About the campground: Located on the grounds of the annual Inter-Tribal Ceremonial gathering, this park is operated by the city of Gallup and makes an ideal stopover for travelers crossing the state on I-40. The facilities are adequate, and the surrounding sculptured red rock formations and cliffs provide a postcard setting.

Grants

Grants is the oasis in the desert of western New Mexico and has a mixed history of logging, mining, railroading, and pure Wild West. Positioned in the shadow of 11,000-foot Mount Taylor, the city is a perfect place from which to venture off I-40 to the north or south. The campgrounds here aren't always crowded, the scenery and activities match those found anywhere in the state, and the fish are just begging to be caught.

After you've caught your limit, area attractions include the Bandera Crater and Ice Caves, El Malpais National Monument, Acoma "Sky City" Pueblo, and the New Mexico Museum of Mining.

For more information:
Grants Chamber of Commerce
PO Box 297
Grants, NM 87020
(800) 748-2142
www.grants.org

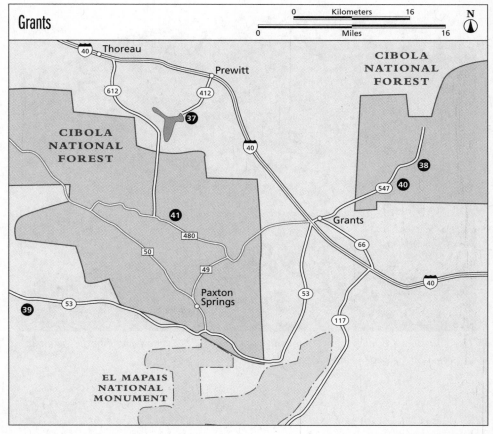

This mist-shrouded hilltop near Mount Taylor is typical of the scenery found in the mountainous regions of far-western New Mexico.

	Group sites	RV sites	Total # of sites	Max. RV length	Hookups	Toilets	Showers	Drinking water	Dump station	Pets	Wheelchair	Recreation	Fee	Season	Can reserve	Stay limit
37	Bluewater Lake State Park	•	•	149		E	F	•	•	•	•		HFBRL	$$$		•	14
38	Coal Mine Canyon	•		15	22		V		•		•		H	$$	May–Sept		14
39	El Morro NM			9			F		•		•		H	$$			14
40	Lobo Canyon	•		9			V		•				H	$	May–Sept		14
41	Ojo Redondo		•	14	20		V				•		HO	$$			14

Hookups: W = Water, E = Electric, S = Sewer
Toilets: F = Flush, V = Vault, P = Pit, C = Chemical
Recreation: H = Hiking, S = Swimming, F = Fishing, B = Boating, L = Boat Launch, O = Off-Highway Driving,
  R = Horseback Riding
Fee (per-night campsite cost): $ = $0 to $5; $$ = $6 to $10; $$$ = $11 to $20.
Maximum Trailer/RV length given in feet. Stay limit given in days. If no entry under Maximum RV length where RV sites are
  available, no restriction is in place.
If no entry under Season, campground is open all year. If no entry under Fee, camping is free.

37 Bluewater Lake State Park

Location: 28 miles northwest of Grants
GPS: N35 17.983' / W108 06.517'
Sites: 149 sites for tents and RVs
Facilities: Flush toilets, tables, grills, group sites, dump station, showers, drinking water, and boat launch
Fee: $ to $$$, annual permit available
Elevation: 7,400 feet
Management: New Mexico State Parks Department; (505) 876-2391; www.emnrd.state.nm.us/SPD/bluewaterlakestatepark.html
Reservations: Call (877) 664-7787; http://newmexicostateparks.reserveamerica.com
Activities: Hiking, fishing, boating, and horseback riding
Season: Year-round
Finding the campground: From I-40 west of Grants, take exit 63. Travel south on NM 412 about 6 miles to the park.
About the campground: Bluewater is aptly named. The cool waters attract visitors seeking relief from the summer heat, making this a very popular campground. The campsites are often filled to capacity, but reservations can ensure you a choice spot. Water sports are a popular pastime at Bluewater, so bring your skis and sailboard.

The campsites, which are scattered near the shore among piñons and juniper trees, have sheltered picnic tables and plenty of space.

38 Coal Mine Canyon

Location: 10 miles northeast of Grants
GPS: N35 14.019' / W107 42.087'
Sites: 15 sites for tents and RVs
Facilities: Vault toilets, tables, grills, and drinking water
Fee: $$
Elevation: 7,400 feet
Management: Cibola National Forest, Mt. Taylor Ranger District; (505) 287-8833
Reservations: Call (877) 444-6777; www.reserveamerica.com; fee
Activities: Hiking and scenic driving
Season: May through September
Finding the campground: From Grants go north on Lobo Canyon Road (NM 547) about 10 miles to the campground.
About the campground: Want to camp on the side of Mount Taylor? Here's your chance. Coal Mine offers all the comforts of developed camping in the Cibola National Forest, and primitive camping is possible throughout this region of the Cibola as well. Either choice is fine if all you want to do is get away from the crowds.

39 El Morro National Monument

Location: 50 miles southwest of Grants
GPS: N35 02.204' / W108 20.270'
Sites: 9 sites for tents
Facilities: Flush toilets, tables, grills, drinking water, visitor center, museum, and hiking trails
Fee: $$
Elevation: 7,200 feet
Management: National Parks Service; (505) 783-4226, ext. 800; www.nps.gov/elmo
Reservations: None
Activities: Hiking
Season: Year-round
Finding the campground: From Grants travel south and then west about 50 miles on NM 53 to the campground.
About the campground: El Morro is a shrine to graffiti: A single sandstone mesa rises like a pinnacle from the desert floor emblazoned with the signs of travelers spanning the centuries. From prehistoric man to the US Army Camel Corps, they all left their mark. As at many national monuments, camping comforts are minimal. The emphasis is on enjoying the history and setting. If you enjoy either, this is the place for you.

40 Lobo Canyon

Location: 9 miles northeast of Grants
GPS: N35 12.222' / W107 42.900'
Sites: 9 sites for tents
Facilities: Vault toilets, tables, and grills
Fee: $
Elevation: 7,400 feet
Management: Cibola National Forest, Mt. Taylor Ranger District; (505) 287-8833
Reservations: None
Activities: Hiking and scenic driving
Season: May through September
Finding the campground: From Grants go north on Lobo Canyon Road (NM 547) about 9 miles to FR 193 Turn south and go 1 mile to the campground.
About the campground: These nine sites are just one more chance to spend the night in this rather secluded area of the Cibola National Forest. The crowds aren't usually a problem, except perhaps locals on picnics. Spend the day watching the wildlife or traveling the numerous forest roads that crisscross the area. (They are slippery when wet!)

Lobo Canyon also makes a convenient place to camp and make day trips to the major attractions of the area.

41 Ojo Redondo

Location: 17 miles southwest of Grants
GPS: N35 09.510' / W108 06.510'
Sites: 14 sites for tents and RVs
Facilities: Vault toilets, tables, and grills
Fee: $$
Elevation: 8,900 feet
Management: Cibola National Forest, Mt. Taylor Ranger District; (505) 287-8833
Reservations: None
Activities: Hiking and scenic driving
Season: Year-round
Finding the campground: From Grants travel south 10 miles on FR 49 (Zuni Canyon Road). Turn west onto FR 480 and go 7 miles to the campground.
About the campground: If you like to get far away from the crowds, then this campground is for you. Getting here won't be easy, but it is a gorgeous drive that winds through piñon-covered canyons dotted by stray lava flows. Enjoy the ride.

Albuquerque

To say that Albuquerque has it all is an understatement. It is the population center of the state and has the usual attractions of a big city with the added bonus of being located in the shadow of 10,000-foot Sandia Peak. It is unfortunate that there are no camping facilities in the Sandia Mountains, but day trips are easily accomplished from the existing campgrounds farther south. A trip to Sandia Crest, whether by car or tram, is a must for visitors to the Albuquerque area. It affords non-hikers the unequaled thrill of standing on a windswept mountaintop.

Public camping in the area is all southeast of the city in the Manzano Mountains. These mountains may lack the grandeur of the Sandias, but they still present hikers, campers, and even equestrians with the opportunity to explore this region of the Cibola National Forest.

For more information:
Albuquerque Convention and Visitor's Bureau
PO Box 26866
Albuquerque, NM 87125-6866
(800) 284-2282
www.visitalbuquerque.org

		Group sites	RV sites	Total # of sites	Max. RV length	Hookups	Toilets	Showers	Drinking water	Dump station	Pets	Wheelchair	Recreation	Fee	Season	Can reserve	Stay limit
42	Capilla Peak	•		8	16		V				•		HR	$	May–Sept		14
43	Manzano Mountains SP	•	•	23		E	F		•	•	•	•	HR	$-$$		•	14
44	New Canyon		•	10	22		V		•		•		H	$	Apr–Nov		14
45	Red Canyon		•	50			V		•		•		HR	$	Apr–Nov		14
46	Red Cloud			4	22		V				•		H		Apr–Oct		14
47	Tajique			6			V		•		•		H		May–Oct		14

Hookups: W = Water,   E = Electric,   S = Sewer
Toilets: F = Flush,   V = Vault,   P = Pit,   C = Chemical
Recreation: H = Hiking,   S = Swimming,   F = Fishing,   B = Boating,   L = Boat Launch,   O = Off-Highway Driving,
   R = Horseback Riding
Fee (per-night campsite cost): $ = $0 to $5; $$ = $6 to $10; $$$ = $11 to $20.
Maximum Trailer/RV length given in feet. Stay limit given in days. If no entry under Maximum RV length where RV sites are available, no restriction is in place.
If no entry under Season, campground is open all year. If no entry under Fee, camping is free.

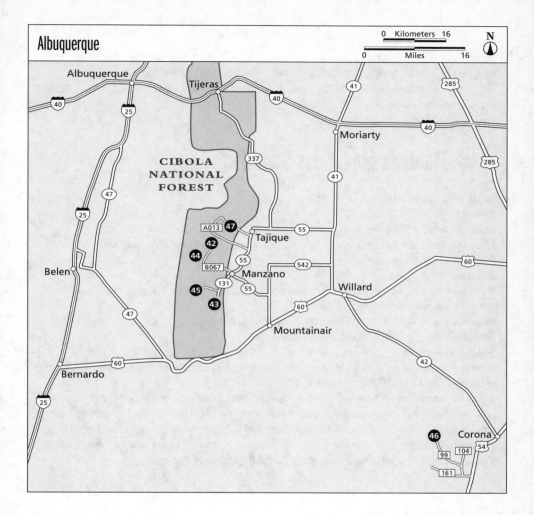

42 **Capilla Peak**

Location: 12 miles west of Manzano
GPS: N34 41.887' / W106 24.101'
Sites: 8 sites for tents and RVs
Facilities: Vault toilets, tables, and grills
Fee: $
Elevation: 9,200 feet
Management: Cibola National Forest, Mountainair Ranger District; (505) 847-2990
Reservations: None
Activities: Hiking and horseback riding
Season: May through September
Finding the campground: From the town of Manzano on NM 55, turn northwest onto CR B066 and go 0.25 mile. Turn north onto B066 and go 0.75 mile. Turn west onto B067 and go 7.5 miles to the campground.

About the campground: Like other campgrounds in the Manzanos, Capilla Peak is primarily designed as a hiking access to the Manzano Wilderness. Trails lead right from camp. Capilla Peak is a bit less accessible than the other camps in the area, so if you're looking for a private hideout, this could be the place.

43 Manzano Mountains State Park

Location: 13 miles northwest of Mountainair
GPS: N34 36.216' / W106 21.656'
Sites: 23 sites for tents and RVs
Facilities: Flush toilets, tables, grills, dump station, electricity, group site, drinking water, and trails
Fee: $ to $$, annual permit available
Elevation: 7,600 feet
Management: New Mexico State Parks Department; (505) 847-2820; www.emnrd.state.nm.us/SPD/manzanomountainsstatepark.html
Reservations: Call (877) 664-7787; http://newmexicostateparks.reserveamerica.com
Activities: Hiking, biking, and horseback riding
Season: Year-round
Finding the campground: From Mountainair travel north 10 miles on NM 55 to Manzano. Turn south onto NM 131/CRB062 and go about 3.25 miles to the park.
About the campground: If you're longing to enjoy a trek in the Manzanos but prefer a few creature comforts, this is the campground for you. The park offers the only electrical hookup sites and the only RV dump station in the region. All of the sites are well spaced among piñon and juniper trees, and the facilities are maintained in the typical state park fashion. The park also has its own set of trails in addition to nearby national forest trails into the Manzano Wilderness.

44 New Canyon

Location: 8 miles west of Manzano
GPS: N34 40.237' / W106 24.568'
Sites: 10 sites for tents and RVs
Facilities: Vault toilets, tables, grills, and drinking water
Fee: $
Elevation: 7,800 feet
Management: Cibola National Forest, Mountainair Ranger District; (505) 847-2990
Reservations: None
Activities: Hiking
Season: April through November
Finding the campground: From the town of Manzano on NM 55, turn northwest onto CR B066 and go 0.25 mile. Turn north onto B066 and go 0.75 mile. Turn west onto B067 and go 4 miles to the campground.
About the campground: This is hiker's heaven. The drawing card here is proximity to both the

Manzano Crest Trail and the Osha Peak Trail. It would not be difficult to spend a full week exploring the Manzano Wilderness from this camp.

45 Red Canyon

Location: 15 miles northwest of Mountainair
GPS: N34 37.270' / W106 24.584'
Sites: 50 sites for tents and RVs
Facilities: Vault toilets, tables, grills, and drinking water
Fee: $
Elevation: 8,000 feet
Management: Cibola National Forest, Mountainair Ranger District; (505) 847-2990
Reservations: None
Activities: Hiking and horseback riding
Season: April through November
Finding the campground: From Mountainair travel north 10 miles on NM 55 to Manzano. Turn south onto NM 131 and go about 2.5 miles. Turn west onto FR 253 and go 2.75 miles to the campground.
About the campground: Load up the horses; this is the place to bring them. An entire section of this large campground is devoted to equestrian use. Corrals are located next to each campsite. Nearby Red Canyon and Spruce Canyon trails allow horseback traffic into the Manzano Wilderness.

Red Canyon is a lovely campground even if you don't have a horse. The pine trees tower over well-spaced sites with modern facilities. Overall, this is probably the nicest camp in the Manzanos.

46 Red Cloud

Location: 18 miles southwest of Corona
GPS: N34 12.621' / W105 45.350'
Sites: 4 sites for tents
Facilities: Vault toilets, tables, and grills
Fee: None
Elevation: 7,900 feet
Management: Cibola National Forest, Mountainair Ranger District; (505) 847-2990
Reservations: None
Activities: Hiking and rock collecting
Season: April through October
Finding the campground: From Corona travel south 11 miles on US 54. Turn west onto FR 161 and go 1 mile. Turn north onto FR 99 and go 8 miles to the campground.
About the campground: Unless you are a hunter, a rockhound, or an old miner, you've probably never heard of Red Cloud. Located near an old mining district, this isolated camp is just the place if your intention is to escape the entire world. With only four developed sites, you aren't likely to

find any other occupants other than during deer hunting season. Bring a lounge chair and a few good books to read and you've got your own slice of heaven in the pines.

47 Tajique

Location: 30 miles south of Tijeras
GPS: N34 45.953' / W106 19.668'
Sites: 6 sites for tents
Facilities: Vault toilets, tables, and grills
Fee: None
Elevation: 6,800 feet
Management: Cibola National Forest, Mountainair Ranger District; (505) 847-2990
Reservations: None
Activities: Hiking
Season: May through October
Finding the campground: From I-40 in Tijeras take exit 175. Go south 24 miles on NM 337. Turn west onto NM 55 and go 2.5 miles to the town of Tajique. Turn west onto FR 55 and go 3 miles to the campground.
About the campground: If the reason you're camping in the Manzanos is to partake of all that Albuquerque has to offer, this is the best campground to choose. It has the easiest access to I-40 and isn't likely to be filled with hikers, who generally choose the higher camps first. It's not a bad place to hang your hat while enjoying one of the Southwest's finest cities.

Northeast

With resort towns like Raton, Red River, and Taos, the northeast is the busy play-ground of the state. The campgrounds are often crowded, but the beauty of the Sangre de Cristos envelops you, drowning out the roar of the crowd. Crystal-clear streams are plentiful, and the wildlife is abundant. As in most of the state, history is one of the top attractions here. The towns are rich with historical cultures—Spanish, Native American, and Mexican. Spend even a little time here and you'll begin to understand why New Mexico is called "the Land of Enchantment."

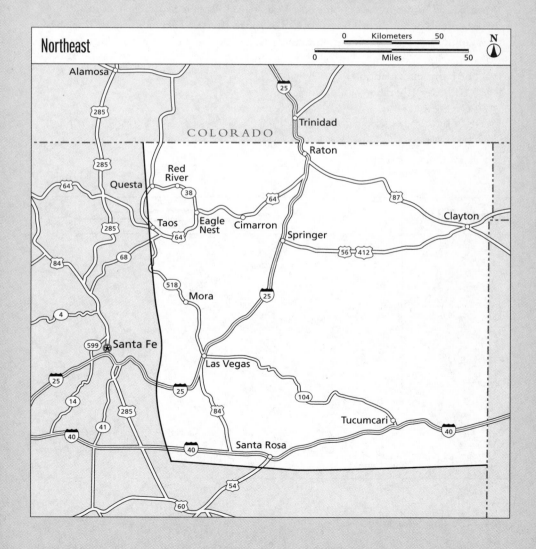

Questa–Red River

There are plenty of jokes about Texans and Red River. Most of them are funny; many of them are even true. But one saying that sums up the relationship best is "Ten thousand Texans can't be wrong." The two key points in that phrase are that on any given weekend you'll likely find Texans by the thousands in the area and all of them have chosen one of the most enjoyable areas of the state to call their second home.

Red River and the surrounding area have good food, nightlife, family entertainment, scenery, trophy fly fishing, hiking to suit all fitness levels, and almost any other mountain activity you can think of. There are plenty of quiet spots to be found; they just aren't in the campgrounds.

Be advised that the Red River area often has a problem with frontcountry bears. As discussed in the introduction, these bears have lost their natural fear of man. They have come to prefer their dinners packed in an ice chest, so keep yours under lock and key. Follow all posted warnings, and visit with rangers regarding any current warnings.

For more information:
Red River Chamber of Commerce
PO Box 870
Red River, NM 87558
(575) 754-2366
www.redrivernewmex.com

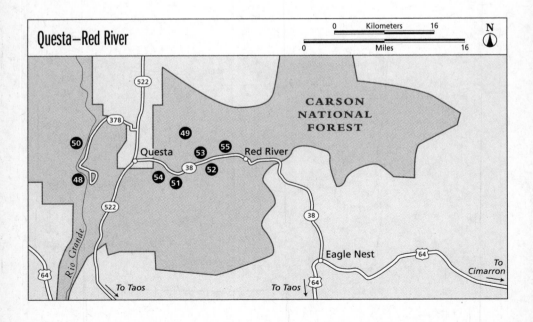

The cool, clear lakes of the northeast region of New Mexico are popular with the fishing crowd.

		Group sites	RV sites	Total # of sites	Max. RV length	Hookups	Toilets	Showers	Drinking water	Dump station	Pets	Wheelchair	Recreation	Fee	Season	Can reserve	Stay limit
48	Big Arsenic Spring			D	22		V		·		·		HF	$$			14
49	Cabresto Lake			9			V				·		HF	$$	May–Sept		14
50	Chiflo			D	22		V		·		·		HF	$$			14
51	Columbine	·		27			V		·		·		HF	$$	May–Oct		14
52	Elephant Rock	·		22			V		·		·		HF	$$	May–Oct		14
53	Fawn Lakes	·		22	32		V		·		·		HF	$$	May–Oct	·	14
54	Goat Hill			3			V				·		F	$$	May–Sept		14
55	Junebug	·		11			V		·		·		F	$$	May–Oct		14

Hookups: W = Water, E = Electric, S = Sewer

Toilets: F = Flush, V = Vault, P = Pit, C = Chemical

Recreation: H = Hiking, S = Swimming, F = Fishing, B = Boating, L = Boat Launch, O = Off-Highway Driving,
    R = Horseback Riding

Fee (per-night campsite cost): $ = $0 to $5; $$ = $6 to $10; $$$ = $11 to $20.

Maximum Trailer/RV length given in feet. Stay limit given in days. If no entry under Maximum RV length where RV sites are
    available, no restriction is in place.

If no entry under Season, campground is open all year. If no entry under Fee, camping is free.

48 Big Arsenic Spring

Location: 10.5 miles southwest of Questa
GPS: N36 40.512' / W105 40.857'
Sites: Dispersed
Facilities: Vault toilets, tables, grills, and drinking water
Fee: $$
Elevation: 6,500 feet
Management: Bureau of Land Management; (575) 758-8851; www.blm.gov/nm
Reservations: None
Activities: Hiking, fishing, biking, and whitewater sports
Season: Year-round
Finding the campground: From Questa travel north 2 miles on NM 522. Turn west onto NM 378 and go 8.5 miles to the campground.
About the campground: This is one of seven developed campgrounds that make up the Bureau of Land Management's Wild Rivers Recreation Area. The area includes the confluence of the Red River and the Rio Grande and is a favorite for fly fishermen, hikers, and whitewater enthusiasts, as well as outdoor photographers and wildlife watchers.

The plunging 1,000-foot cliffs that line the Rio Grande at the Rio Grande Gorge mark the southernmost point in the Wild Rivers Recreation Area, with the area extending north more than 20 miles. Camping at all of the campgrounds is on a first-come, first-served basis, but well worth the hassle of getting there early to secure a site.

49 Cabresto Lake

Location: 6 miles northeast of Questa
GPS: N36 44.802' / W105 29.950'
Sites: 9 sites for tents
Facilities: Vault toilets, tables, and grills
Fee: $$
Elevation: 9,200 feet
Management: Carson National Forest, Questa Ranger District; (575) 586-0520
Reservations: None
Activities: Hiking and fishing
Season: May through September
Finding the campground: From Questa travel northeast 5 miles on FR 134 to the campground access.
About the campground: Just try to describe the setting here without clichés. You can't talk about Cabresto Lake without using the words "breathtaking" or "serene." The only problem here is the road, which borders on being four-wheel drive. No trailers are allowed. If you get to Cabresto, attempt the 4-mile hike to Heart Lake, but go prepared because the cold will take you by surprise. Even a partial hike on this trail is worth the effort because the surroundings are so . . . um . . . okay, breathtaking.

The northern water of the Rio Grande has only a few calm places.

50 Chiflo

Location: 7.5 miles northwest of Questa
GPS: N36 44.454' / W105 40.765'
Sites: Dispersed
Facilities: Vault toilets, tables, grills, and drinking water
Fee: $$
Elevation: 7,600 feet
Management: US Bureau of Land Management; (505) 758-8851; www.blm.gov/nm
Reservations: None
Activities: Hiking, fishing, biking, and whitewater sports
Season: Year-round
Finding the campground: From Questa travel north 2 miles on NM 522. Turn west onto NM 378 and go 5.5 miles to the campground.
About the campground: Chiflo is part of the Wild Rivers Recreation Area. See description at site 48, Big Arsenic Spring.

51 Columbine

Location: 4.5 miles east of Questa
GPS: N36 40.883' / W105 30.926'
Sites: 27 sites for tents and RVs
Facilities: Vault toilets, tables, grills, and drinking water
Fee: $$
Elevation: 7,900 feet
Management: Carson National Forest, Questa Ranger District; (575) 586-0520
Reservations: None
Activities: Hiking and fishing
Season: May through October
Finding the campground: From Questa travel 4.5 miles east on NM 38 to the campground.
About the campground: Besides being a lovely place from which to enjoy all the treats of the Red River area, Columbine provides access to the Columbine-Twinning Trail, which crosses the Taos Mountains at more than 12,000 feet. Attempting the entire journey should be left up to serious hikers, but the rest of us can certainly enjoy a few miles up and back along this incredible trail.

52 Elephant Rock

Location: 3 miles west of Red River
GPS: N36 42.358' / W105 27.342'
Sites: 22 sites for tents and RVs

Facilities: Vault toilets, tables, grills, and drinking water
Fee: $$
Elevation: 8,300 feet
Management: Carson National Forest, Questa Ranger District; (575) 586-0520
Reservations: None
Activities: Hiking and fishing
Season: May through October
Finding the campground: From Red River travel west 3 miles on NM 38 to the campground.
About the campground: As with the other roadside campgrounds along NM 38 between Red River and Questa, the main idea here is to have access to all those trout in the Red River and still be close enough to town to enjoy a night of dining and dancing. Elephant Rock fits the bill. Currently, none of the campgrounds on NM 38 are on the National Recreation Reservation System, but it would not hurt to check. Call (877) 444-6777.

53 Fawn Lakes

Location: 3.5 miles west of Red River
GPS: N36 42.352' / W105 27.400'
Sites: 22 sites for tents and RVs
Facilities: Vault toilets, tables, grills, and drinking water
Fee: $$
Elevation: 8,500 feet
Management: Carson National Forest, Questa Ranger District; (575) 586-0520
Reservations: Call (877) 444-6777; www.reserveamerica.com
Activities: Hiking, fishing, and biking
Season: May through October
Finding the campground: From Red River travel west 3.5 miles on NM 38 to the campground.
About the campground: Fawn Lakes is on the north side of NM 38 and provides fishing access to two stocked ponds. This makes it an ideal destination for those who prefer stillwater fishing over stream fishing. You can expect modern facilities here.

54 Goat Hill

Location: 4 miles east of Questa
GPS: N36 41.285' / W105 32.434'
Sites: 3 sites for tents
Facilities: Vault toilets, tables, and grills
Fee: $$
Elevation: 7,700 feet
Management: Carson National Forest, Questa Ranger District; (575) 586-0520
Reservations: None
Activities: Fishing

Season: May through September

Finding the campground: From Questa travel 4 miles east on NM 38 to the campground.

About the campground: If you can get a spot, this tiny camp is ideal for those looking to fish the Red River but who disdain the larger, busier campgrounds. The fact that it is the farthest camp from Red River also helps to thin the crowd. Give it a try during midweek, and you'll probably be alone.

55 Junebug

Location: 2 miles west of Red River

GPS: N36 42.468' / W105 26.084'

Sites: 11 sites for tents and RVs

Facilities: Vault toilets, tables, grills, and drinking water

Fee: $$

Elevation: 8,500 feet

Management: Carson National Forest, Questa Ranger District; (575) 586-0520

Reservations: None

Activities: Fishing

Season: May through October

Finding the campground: From Red River travel 2 miles west on NM 38 to the campground.

About the campground: Junebug is as close to town as you can camp, so expect ten thousand Texans to be vying for these choice sites. If you can catch it either early or late in the season before the crowds hit, this is a pleasant little camp.

Cimarron–Eagle Nest

For many New Mexico visitors, this area is practically a second home. The fishing at Eagle Nest Lake is ranked among the best in the state, the scenic drive through Cimarron Canyon is one you will not want to miss, and the hiking is ideal for all levels of trekkers. Rock collectors and geology buffs traverse the area known as the Palisades in search of agate and minerals, while wildlife enthusiasts are rarely disappointed in the abundance of flora and fauna found in the region.

Also, you are just around the bend from the bustling activity of Red River. The only drawback here is the crowded conditions. But if you don't mind bumping shoulders with fellow outdoor types, come on down.

For more information:
Cimarron Chamber of Commerce
PO Box 604
Cimarron, NM 87714
(575) 376–2417
www.cimarronnm.com

Winter months bring heavy snowfalls and out-of-state skiers.
Juan Benevides

Eagle Nest Chamber of Commerce
284 E. Therma Dr.
Eagle Nest, NM 87718
(575) 377-2420
www.eaglenestchamber.org

	Group sites	RV sites	Total # of sites	Max. RV length	Hookups	Toilets	Showers	Drinking water	Dump station	Pets	Wheelchair	Recreation	Fee	Season	Can reserve	Stay limit
56	**Cimarron Canyon SP**		•	94			V		•		•	•	HFR	$-$$			14
57	**Cimarron**		•	36	32		V				•		HFR	$$	May–Oct	•	14
58	**McCrystal**		•	60			V		•		•		HFR		May–Oct		14

Hookups: W = Water,   E = Electric,   S = Sewer

Toilets: F = Flush,   V = Vault,   P = Pit,   C = Chemical

Recreation: H = Hiking,   S = Swimming,   F = Fishing,   B = Boating,   L = Boat Launch,   O = Off-Highway Driving,   R = Horseback Riding

Fee (per-night campsite cost): $ = $0 to $5; $$ = $6 to $10; $$$ = $11 to $20.

Maximum Trailer/RV length given in feet. Stay limit given in days. If no entry under Maximum RV length where RV sites are available, no restriction is in place.

If no entry under Season, campground is open all year. If no entry under Fee, camping is free.

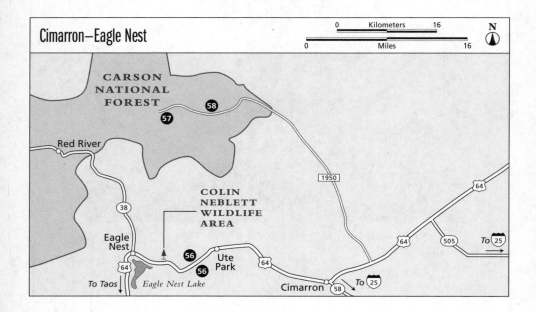

Cimarron–Eagle Nest

56 Cimarron Canyon State Park

Location: 7.5 miles east of Eagle Nest
GPS: N36 32.045' / W105 09.953'
Sites: 94 sites for tents and RVs, divided among 4 campgrounds
Facilities: Vault toilets, tables, grills, and drinking water; wheelchair-accessible facilities

Fee: $ to $$, annual permit available
Elevation: 8,000 feet
Management: New Mexico State Parks Department; (575) 377-6271; www.emnrd.state.nm.us/SPD/cimarroncanyonstatepark.html
Reservations: None
Activities: Hiking, fishing, rock collecting, scenic driving, biking, and horseback riding
Season: Year-round
Finding the campground: From Eagle Nest travel east 7.5 miles on US 64 to the campgrounds.
About the campground: Cimarron Canyon State Park is part of the Colin-Neblett Wildlife Area, the largest in the state and through which traverse trails suitable for hiking, biking, and horseback riding. The canyon itself presents a wealth of opportunities for exploring. Trailheads are found along US 64 throughout the park, including two that take you up to the incredible Palisades rock formations.

There are two trailer campgrounds in the park, Maverick (formerly called Gravel Pit Lakes) and Ponderosa. Both are nice camps in ponderosa pine forest, but with somewhat narrow spacing of sites. Keep in mind that these campgrounds fill quickly, so don't expect to pull in at midnight Friday and find a spot. Also, remember to practice bear-safe camping, because during most seasons the area has black furry visitors on a nightly basis.

57 Cimarron

Location: 40 miles northwest of Cimarron
GPS: N36 46.168' / W105 12.300'
Sites: 36 sites for tents and RVs
Facilities: Vault toilets, tables, and grills
Fee: $$
Elevation: 9,400 feet
Management: Carson National Forest, Questa Ranger District; (575) 586-0520
Reservations: Call (877) 444-6777; www.reserveamerica.com
Activities: Hiking, fishing, and horseback riding
Season: May through October
Finding the campground: From Cimarron travel east 1.25 miles on US 64. Turn northwest onto NM 204 and go 20.5 miles. Turn north onto FR 1910 and go 6 miles to the campground.
About the campground: It's always odd to find such a large campground so far from everything. Cimarron and the neighboring McCrystal are popular, but not in the way the campgrounds in Cimarron Canyon are. The pace here is slower and the atmosphere quieter, probably because everyone who travels this far on gravel and dirt roads is serious about getting away from the rest of the world. Nine of the sites are equestrian.

Fishing and additional unimproved sites are available on nearby Shuree Ponds, but the main attraction here besides the scenery is the elk. The Valle Vidal area of the Carson National Forest is known throughout the Southwest for its ever-increasing herd, so bring your binoculars.

58 McCrystal

Location: 35 miles northwest of Cimarron
GPS: N36 46.619' / W105 06.833'
Sites: 60 sites for tents and RVs
Facilities: Vault toilets, tables, grills, and drinking water
Fee: None
Elevation: 8,100 feet
Management: Carson National Forest, Questa Ranger District; (575) 586-0520
Reservations: None
Activities: Hiking, fishing, and horseback riding
Season: May through October
Finding the campground: From Cimarron travel east 5.1 miles on US 64. Turn north onto FR 1950 and go 30 miles to the campground.
About the campground: McCrystal is another example of what a national forest campground can and should be: a place to retreat from the world into a setting that affords the opportunity to enjoy the grandeur of nature. Although there are 60 sites here, they are well spaced and, as at neighboring Cimarron, most of your fellow campers here will be conscientious outdoors people.

Clayton-Raton-Springer

The northeastern corner of New Mexico is a prelude to the grander things to come as you near the Rocky Mountains. Massive volcanic craters jut from the plains, teasing the horizon. Desert mesas slowly give way to piñon-covered mountains. Though sparsely populated by humans, the triangle between Clayton, Raton, and Springer is abundant with desert wildlife. Herds of pronghorn antelope sprint across the prairies in what is one of the few untouched areas of the Great Plains. People who pass through here are often too busy rushing north or west to appreciate the beauty, but those who slow down are well rewarded.

For more information:
Clayton/Union County Chamber of Commerce
1103 S. First St.
PO Box 476
Clayton, NM 88415
(575) 374-9253
www.claytonnm.org

Raton Chamber of Commerce
100 Clayton Rd.
Raton, NM 87740
(575) 445-3689
www.raton.info

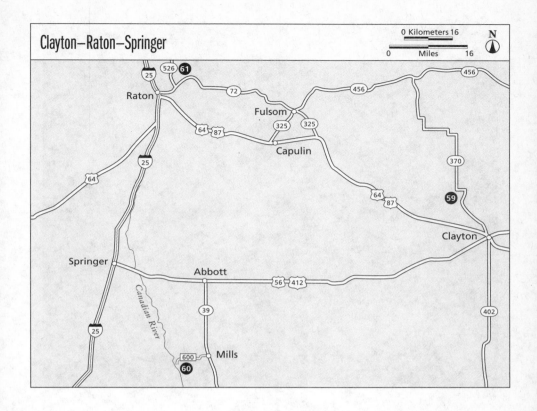

Clayton–Raton–Springer

Hookups: W = Water,　E = Electric,　S = Sewer

Toilets: F = Flush,　V = Vault,　P = Pit,　C = Chemical

Recreation: H = Hiking,　S = Swimming,　F = Fishing,　B = Boating,　L = Boat Launch,　O = Off-Highway Driving,
　　R = Horseback Riding

Fee (per-night campsite cost): $ = $0 to $5;　$$ = $6 to $10;　$$$ = $11 to $20.

Maximum Trailer/RV length given in feet. Stay limit given in days. If no entry under Maximum RV length where RV sites are
　　available, no restriction is in place.

If no entry under Season, campground is open all year. If no entry under Fee, camping is free.

		Group sites	RV sites	Total # of sites	Max. RV length	Hookups	Toilets	Showers	Drinking water	Dump station	Pets	Wheelchair	Recreation	Fee	Season	Can reserve	Stay limit
59	Clayton Lake State Park	·	·	26		WE	F		·	·	·	·	HFBL	$-$$			14
60	Mills Canyon			D			V						H				14
61	Sugarite Canyon State Park	·	·	40		E	F		·	·	·	·	HFBL	$-$$		·	14

Wildflowers dot the hillsides and roadways in this region of the state in late spring.

Springer Chamber of Commerce
PO Box 323
Springer, NM 87747
http://springerchamberofcommerce.org

59 Clayton Lake State Park

Location: 15 miles northwest of Clayton
GPS: N36 34.393' / W103 18.070'
Sites: 26 sites for tents and RVs
Facilities: Flush toilets, showers, tables, grills, dump station, playground, boat launch, and hiking trails; wheelchair-accessible facilities
Fee: $ to $$, annual permit available
Elevation: 5,100 feet
Management: New Mexico State Parks Department; (575) 374-8808; www.emnrd.state.nm.us/SPD/claytonlakestatepark.html
Reservations: None
Activities: Hiking, fishing, and boating
Season: Year-round
Finding the campground: From Clayton travel northwest 9 miles on NM 370. Turn west onto NM 455 and go 2 miles to the park.
About the campground: Besides the fishing and the lazy high-plains atmosphere, Clayton Lake offers a rare opportunity to view easily discernible dinosaur tracks captured in the mud of ancient watering holes. There are interpretive exhibits and a boardwalk that allows you to walk out over the track site. It's a fascinating adventure that makes a worthwhile side trip, even if you don't plan to camp here. The campground has the comforts of most New Mexico state parks.

60 Mills Canyon

Location: 42 miles southeast of Springer
GPS: N36 02.852' / W104 22.632'
Sites: Dispersed, tents only
Facilities: Vault toilets
Fee: None
Elevation: 5,100 feet
Management: Kiowa National Grasslands; (575) 374-9652
Reservations: None
Activities: Hiking and wildlife watching
Season: Year-round
Finding the campground: From Springer travel 18 miles east on US 56 to Abbott. Turn south onto NM 39 and go 16.5 miles. Turn west onto CR U1 (which becomes FR 600) and go 8 miles to the canyon.
About the campground: This is primitive camping at its finest in lowland New Mexico. Tent camping is possible at the canyon rim, but the choice spots are at the end of a 2-mile trail that drops the last 800 feet into the canyon. The road getting here is bad when dry and impassable when wet. High-clearance vehicles are recommended. This campground serves as a reminder that the good things in life are always at the end of the roughest roads.

61 Sugarite Canyon State Park

Location: 10 miles northeast of Raton
GPS coordinates: N36 57.545' / W104 23.165'
Sites: 40 sites for tents and RVs
Facilities: Flush toilets, visitor center, group sites, electricity, tables, grills, drinking water, dump station, showers, hiking trails, and boat launch; wheelchair-accessible facilities
Fee: $ to $$, annual permit available
Elevation: 7,800 feet
Management: New Mexico State Parks Department; (575) 445-5607; www.emnrd.state.nm.us/SPD/sugaritecanyonstatepark.html
Reservations: None
Activities: Hiking, fishing, boating, and scenic driving
Season: Year-round
Finding the campground: From I-25 take exit 452 in Raton. Turn east onto NM 72 and go 3 miles. Turn north onto NM 526 and go 2 miles to the park.
About the campground: Sugarite is a world all its own, tucked away in the hills outside Raton. Few other than New Mexican locals even know it exists. The setting includes pine-covered hillsides and rolling mountain meadows. If you can include this park in your New Mexico itinerary, you won't be disappointed.

Tucumcari

Curled beneath the colorful mesa known as Tucumcari Mountain, this New Mexico gateway city still thrives on the memory of US Route 66. The town is quaint and has all the conveniences. And some of the state's best water sports areas are just a stone's throw away.

For more information:
Tucumcari–Quay County Chamber of Commerce
404 W. Rte. 66
PO Drawer E
Tucumcari, NM 88401
(575) 461–1694
www.tucumcarinm.com

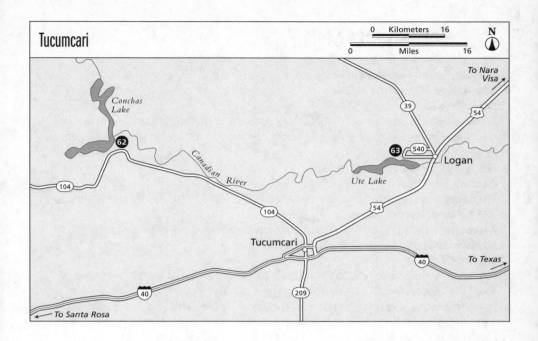

		Group sites	RV sites	Total # of sites	Max. RV length	Hookups	Toilets	Showers	Drinking water	Dump station	Pets	Wheelchair	Recreation	Fee	Season	Can reserve	Stay limit
62	**Conchas Lake State Park**	·	·	105		WE	F	·	·	·	·		HFBL	$-$$		·	14
63	**Ute Lake State Park**	·	·	142		WE	F	·	·	·	·		HFBL	$-$$		·	14

Hookups: W = Water, E = Electric, S = Sewer

Toilets: F = Flush, V = Vault, P = Pit, C = Chemical

Recreation: H = Hiking, S = Swimming, F = Fishing, B = Boating, L = Boat Launch, O = Off-Highway Driving, R = Horseback Riding

Fee (per-night campsite cost): $ = $0 to $5; $$ = $6 to $10; $$$ = $11 to $20.

Maximum Trailer/RV length given in feet. Stay limit given in days. If no entry under Maximum RV length where RV sites are available, no restriction is in place.

If no entry under Season, campground is open all year. If no entry under Fee, camping is free.

62 Conchas Lake State Park

Location: 34 miles northwest of Tucumcari
GPS: N35 22.646' / W104 11.381'
Sites: 105 sites for tents and RVs
Facilities: Flush toilets, visitor center, electricity, dump station, tables, grills, drinking water, showers, marina, playground, hiking trails, boat launch, shelters, and golf course; wheelchair-accessible facilities
Fee: $ to $$, annual permit available
Elevation: 4,200 feet
Management: New Mexico State Parks Department; (575) 868-2270; www.emnrd.state.nm.us/SPD/conchaslakestatepark.html
Reservations: Call (877) 664-7787; http://newmexicostateparks.reserveamerica.com
Activities: Hiking, fishing, water sports, and scuba diving
Season: Year-round
Finding the campground: From Tucumcari travel 34 miles northwest on NM 104 to the park.
About the campground: This is the desert Southwest, so don't expect to use the words "lush" or "green" to describe Conchas. "Colorful" does apply, however. The earth is red, and the sky and water are clear blue. The water is clear enough, in fact, to attract scuba divers almost year-round. It isn't the Caribbean, but treasure hunting is a popular pastime among the divers.

The campgrounds are well maintained, with plenty of space between sites and plenty of parking for boats. As at any body of water in New Mexico, expect crowds during the busy summer season. Conchas Lake is a US Army Corps of Engineers lake, but the campgrounds are managed by the state parks department. Federal recreation passports are not accepted in the state park.

63 Ute Lake State Park

Location: 3 miles west of Logan
GPS: N35 21.611' / W103 27.047'
Sites: 142 sites for tents and RVs
Facilities: Flush toilets, tables, grills, drinking water, visitor center, group sites, electricity, dump station, showers, marina, and hiking trails; wheelchair-accessible facilities
Fee: $ to $$, annual permit available
Elevation: 3,900 feet
Management: New Mexico State Parks Department; (575) 487-2284; www.emnrd.state.nm.us/SPD/utelakestatepark.html
Reservations: Call (877) 664-7787; http://newmexicostateparks.reserveamerica.com
Activities: Hiking, fishing, and boating
Season: Year-round
Finding the campground: From Logan travel 3 miles west on NM 540 to the park.
About the campground: Though considerably smaller than its neighbor Conchas, Ute Lake is popular among bass anglers throughout New Mexico and parts of Texas. The campground is nestled along the shore, with some shade provided by cottonwoods. Expect crowds almost any time of year.

Taos-Pilar

Art, fashion, food, whitewater rafting, and jagged mountain peaks—if you're going to New Mexico in search of anything else, then don't bother with Taos. Save it for the rest of us who thrive on the magic of this place. For over a hundred years, artists and writers have drifted to Taos, and their influence is unmistakable in the city and surrounding area. The mountains near Taos are a work of art in themselves, supplying the best skiing in the state in winter and some of the best climbing and hiking during the rest of the year.

For more information:
Taos County Chamber of Commerce
1139 Paseo del Pueblo Sur
Taos, NM 87571
(575) 751–8800
www.taoschamber.com

		Group sites	RV sites	Total # of sites	Max. RV length	Hookups	Toilets	Showers	Drinking water	Dump station	Pets	Wheelchair	Recreation	Fee	Season	Can reserve	Stay limit
64	Capulin		·	10	16		V		·		·		HF	$$	May-Oct		14
65	Cuchillo de Medio		·	3	16		V				·		F		May-Sept		14
66	La Sombra		·	13	16		V		·		·		HF	$$	May-Oct		14
67	Las Petacas		·	9			V				·		F	$$	Apr-Nov		14
68	Lower Hondo		·	4	16		V				·		F	$$	May-Sept		14
69	Orilla Verde NRA	·		23			V		·		·		HF	$$			14
70	Twining		·	4	16		V				·		FH	$$	May-Sept		14

Hookups: W = Water,   E = Electric,   S = Sewer
Toilets: F = Flush,   V = Vault,   P = Pit,   C = Chemical
Recreation: H = Hiking,   S = Swimming,   F = Fishing,   B = Boating,   L = Boat Launch,   O = Off-Highway Driving,
    R = Horseback Riding
Fee (per-night campsite cost): $ = $0 to $5; $$ = $6 to $10; $$$ = $11 to $20.
Maximum Trailer/RV length given in feet. Stay limit given in days. If no entry under Maximum RV length where RV sites are
    available, no restriction is in place.
If no entry under Season, campground is open all year. If no entry under Fee, camping is free.

The Taos Bridge offers a spectacular view of the Rio Grande Gorge.

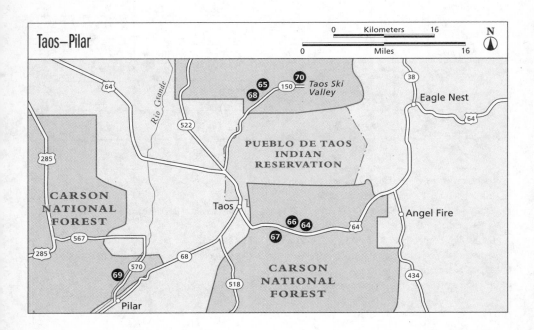

64 Capulin

Location: 6 miles east of Taos
GPS: N36 22.198' / W105 28.863'
Sites: 10 sites for tents and RVs
Facilities: Vault toilets, tables, grills, and drinking water
Fee: $$
Elevation: 8,000 feet
Management: Carson National Forest, Camino Real District; (575) 587-2255
Reservations: None
Activities: Hiking and fishing
Season: May through October
Finding the campground: From Taos travel east 6 miles on US 64 to the campground.
About the campground: Capulin is a pleasant little roadside campground between Taos and Angel Fire. It's a good spot from which to explore the Taos area but will work just as well if you're inclined only to pull out the lawn chairs and do nothing. There's a trail to the nearby Ice Cave waterfall for a bit of added interest. The campground fills quickly.

65 Cuchillo de Medio

Location: 13 miles northeast of Taos
GPS: N36 33.585' / W105 32.000'
Sites: 3 sites for tents and RVs
Facilities: Vault toilets, tables, and grills
Fee: None
Elevation: 7,800 feet
Management: Carson National Forest, Canjilon Ranger District; (575) 684-2489
Reservations: None
Activities: Fishing
Season: May through September
Finding the campground: From Taos travel northwest 3 miles on NM 522. Turn north on NM 230 and go 2.5 miles to NM 150. Turn east and go 7.5 miles to the campground.
About the campground: This is one of four opportunities to camp along the Rio Hondo on the road to the Taos Ski Valley. The problem is that all four camps are tiny, so if this is where you want to be, you'd better get here midweek. The scenery is spectacular and the fishing usually good. Although the campground is small, it's not an ideal spot to escape fellow travelers due to the potential for road noise.

66 La Sombra

Location: 6 miles east of Taos
GPS: N36 22.126' / W105 28.409'
Sites: 13 sites for tents and RVs
Facilities: Vault toilets, tables, grills, and drinking water
Fee: $$
Elevation: 7,800 feet
Management: Carson National Forest, Camino Real Ranger District; (575) 587-2255
Reservations: None
Activities: Hiking and fishing
Season: May through October
Finding the campground: From Taos travel east 6 miles on US 64 to the campground.
About the campground: Camping in Taos Canyon is heaven for those who like convenience to stores, a place to fish, and perfect New Mexican scenery. Keep in mind that everybody else wants a slice of heaven, too, so you have to arrive early to get one of these 13 sites.

67 Las Petacas

Location: 4 miles east of Taos
GPS: N36 22.902' / W105 31.317'
Sites: 9 sites for tents and RVs
Facilities: Vault toilets, tables, and grills
Fee: $$
Elevation: 7,400 feet
Management: Carson National Forest, Camino Real Ranger District; (575) 587-2255
Reservations: None
Activities: Fishing
Season: April through November
Finding the campground: From Taos travel east 4 miles on US 64 to the campground.
About the campground: Las Petacas is the closest public campground to Taos. The pines and cottonwoods of Taos Canyon blend into a shimmering sea of green that begs you to never leave, so bring a hammock and plan to stay a while.

68 Lower Hondo

Location: 11.5 miles northeast of Taos
GPS: N36 32.835' / W105 32.967'
Sites: 4 sites for tents and RVs
Facilities: Vault toilets, tables, and grills

Fee: $$

Elevation: 7,700 feet

Management: Carson National Forest, Camino Real Ranger District; (575) 587-2255

Reservations: None

Activities: Fishing

Season: May through September

Finding the campground: From Taos travel northwest 3 miles on NM 522. Turn north on NM 230 and go 2.5 miles to NM 150. Turn east and go 6.5 miles to the campground.

About the campground: Lower Hondo is the lowest among the string of campgrounds on the Rio Hondo. Primary use is by hikers seeking proximity to the Wheeler Peak Wilderness Area, which borders NM 150. The four sites here make a very nice retreat, if you can find one available.

69 Orilla Verde National Recreation Area

Location: 2 miles north of Pilar

GPS: N36 19.833' / W105 44.751'

Sites: 23 sites for tents

Facilities: Vault toilets, tables, grills, drinking water, and group sites

Fee: $$

Elevation: 6,000 feet

Management: Bureau of Land Management, Taos Field Office; (575) 758-8851; www.blm.gov/nm

Reservations: None

Activities: Hiking and fishing

Season: Year-round

Finding the campground: From Pilar travel north 2 miles on NM 570 to the campground.

About the campground: As part of the US Bureau of Land Management's Wild and Scenic River Project, Orilla provides access to the rushing waters of the Rio Grande. Whitewater sports are the big draw here, but fly fishing is also a popular pastime. If you're willing to come down from campgrounds in the mountains, these campsites along the river are a real treat.

70 Twining

Location: 19 miles northeast of Taos

GPS: N36 35.752' / W105 27.034'

Sites: 4 sites for tents and RVs

Facilities: Vault toilets, tables, and grills

Fee: $$

Elevation: 9,300 feet

Management: Carson National Forest, Camino Real Ranger District; (575) 587-2255

Reservations: None

Activities: Fishing and hiking

Season: May through September

Finding the campground: From Taos travel northwest 3 miles on NM 522. Turn north on NM 230 and go 2.5 miles to NM 150. Turn east and go 12.5 miles to the campground.

About the campground: What would camping near Taos be without the opportunity to experience Wheeler Peak? These four sites at Twining offer the high-country experience at its finest. From here you can hike to your heart's content, and then come back to the comfort of your camp to relive the day's adventure. Just keep in mind that like all campsites near Taos, these are first-come, first-served, so be early.

Tres Ritos

Ask any Texan who camps in New Mexico, and they will be happy to tell you all about Tres Ritos. It has been a favorite for decades. Located deep in the heart of the Sangre de Cristo Mountains, this is the place to escape the traffic noise, the phones, and the rush of the world. Unfortunately, you won't escape the crowd, but there's usually plenty of space for everyone. Fishing is good in several streams and rivers that course through the area, and trail activities like hiking, horseback riding, and mountain biking are all possible from here.

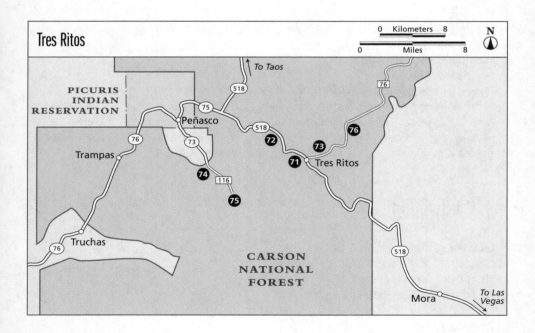

		Group sites	RV sites	Total # of sites	Max. RV length	Hookups	Toilets	Showers	Drinking water	Dump station	Pets	Wheelchair	Recreation	Fee	Season	Can reserve	Stay limit
71	Agua Piedra	·	·	13	32		V		·		·		HFR	$$	May–Oct		14
72	Comales			10			V		·				HFOR	$			
73	Duran Canyon		·	12			V		·		·		HFR	$$	May–Sept		14
74	Hodges			14			V				·		HFR	$	May–Oct		14
75	Santa Barbara		·	12			V		·				HFR	$$	May–Sept		14
76	Upper La Junta		·	8	16		V				·		HF	$	May–Oct		14

Hookups: W = Water, E = Electric, S = Sewer
Toilets: F = Flush, V = Vault, P = Pit, C = Chemical
Recreation: H = Hiking, S = Swimming, F = Fishing, B = Boating, L = Boat Launch, O = Off-Highway Driving,
   R = Horseback Riding
Fee (per-night campsite cost): $ = $0 to $5; $$ = $6 to $10; $$$ = $11 to $20.
Maximum Trailer/RV length given in feet. Stay limit given in days. If no entry under Maximum RV length where RV sites are
   available, no restriction is in place.
If no entry under Season, campground is open all year. If no entry under Fee, camping is free.

71 Agua Piedra

Location: 1.5 miles northwest of Tres Ritos
GPS: N36 08.118' / W105 31.751'
Sites: 13 sites for tents and RVs
Facilities: Vault toilets, tables, grills, and drinking water
Fee: $$
Elevation: 8,400 feet
Management: Carson National Forest, Camino Real Ranger District; (575) 587-2255
Reservations: None
Activities: Hiking, fishing, and horseback riding
Season: May through October
Finding the campground: From Tres Ritos travel 1.5 miles northwest on NM 518 to the
campground.
About the campground: One of the easily accessible campgrounds along NM 518, Agua Piedra
offers fishing access to the Rio Pueblo. The sites are well spaced among the pines, and three
additional primitive sites are located nearby at South Agua Piedra. Bring a hammock because this
place is comfortable. Remember that because it's on the main road, it is more likely to fill quickly.

72 Comales

Location: 7 miles east of Penasco
GPS: N36 09.602' / W105 35.784'
Sites: 10 sites for tents and RVs
Facilities: Vault toilets, tables, and fire rings
Fee: $
Elevation: 7,800 feet
Management: Carson National Forest, Camino Real Ranger District; (575) 587-2255
Reservations: None
Activities: Fishing, hiking, horseback riding, and off-road vehicles
Season: Year-round
Finding the campground: From Penasco travel north and east on NM 75 about 6 miles; then merge onto NM 518 and continue about 2 miles to the campground.
About the campground: Add this to the list of campgrounds from which to explore the Taos region. The town and the Taos Pueblo are only 30 minutes away. You can always choose to while away the hours fishing for trout in the Rio Pueblo, or hike the Comales Canyon Trail.

73 Duran Canyon

Location: 2 miles northeast of Tres Ritos
GPS: N36 08.035' / W105 28.634'
Sites: 12 sites for tents and RVs
Facilities: Vault toilets, tables, grills, and drinking water
Fee: $$
Elevation: 9,000 feet
Management: Carson National Forest, Camino Real Ranger District; (575) 587-2255
Reservations: None
Activities: Hiking, fishing, and horseback riding
Season: May through September
Finding the campground: From Tres Ritos travel 2 miles northeast on FR 76 to the campground.
About the campground: Duran Canyon offers 12 lovely campsites with hiking access to the Pecos Wilderness and fishing in Duran Creek.

74 Hodges

Location: 6 miles southeast of Penasco
GPS: N36 06.936' / W105 38.334'
Sites: 14 sites for tents
Facilities: Vault toilets, tables, and grills

Fee: $
Elevation: 8,000 feet
Management: Carson National Forest, Camino Real Ranger District; (575) 587-2255
Reservations: None
Activities: Hiking, fishing, and horseback riding
Season: May through October
Finding the campground: From Penasco travel 6 miles southeast on FR 116 to the campground.
About the campground: Hodges sometimes serves as an overflow area for the more popular Santa Barbara campground farther down the road, but there's no reason not to make this your intended destination. The surroundings are peaceful, the campground well laid out, and it's a bit more off the beaten track than those closer to Tres Ritos.

75 Santa Barbara

Location: 9 miles southeast of Penasco
GPS: N36 05.135' / W105 36.534'
Sites: 12 sites for tents and RVs
Facilities: Vault toilets, tables, grills, and drinking water
Fee: $$
Elevation: 8,800 feet
Management: Carson National Forest, Camino Real Ranger District; (575) 587-2255
Reservations: None
Activities: Hiking, fishing, and horseback riding
Season: May through September
Finding the campground: From Penasco travel 9 miles southeast on FR 116 to the campground.
About the campground: Santa Barbara is the largest and probably the most popular campground in the Tres Ritos area. With access to the trails leading into the Pecos Wilderness, many use it as a drop-off point for hiking the Truchas-area peaks. Horse corrals are available for trail riders as well.

76 Upper La Junta

Location: 4 miles northeast of Tres Ritos
GPS: N36 08.868' / W105 27.317'
Sites: 8 sites for tents and RVs
Facilities: Vault toilets, tables, and grills
Fee: $
Elevation: 9,000 feet
Management: Carson National Forest, Camino Real Ranger District; (575) 587-2255
Reservations: None
Activities: Hiking, fishing, and mountain biking
Season: May through October
Finding the campground: From Tres Ritos travel 4 miles northeast on FR 76 to the campground.

The Santa Barbara River flows near the Tres Ritos–area campsites.

About the campground: The crowds are a bit thinner here than along the highway below. Fishing access to the Rio La Junta provides plenty of opportunity to catch a trout or two. The camp is also a popular base camp for mountain bikers and dirt bikers (both of which are allowed on nearby trails).

Las Vegas–Mora

Billed as the gateway between the Great Plains and the Rocky Mountains, Las Vegas is an interesting mix of genuine New Mexican culture and tourist glitz. You won't find as much artiness here, nor as many tourists, as in Santa Fe or Taos. This works to your advantage if you're looking for someplace a bit quieter. The mountains west of here are every bit as beautiful as those deeper in the heart of the state, so you won't be disappointed in these campgrounds.

For more information:
Las Vegas/San Miguel County Chamber of Commerce
1224 Railroad Ave.
Las Vegas, NM 87701
(505) 425-8631
www.lasvegasnewmexico.com

		Group sites	RV sites	Total # of sites	Max. RV length	Hookups	Toilets	Showers	Drinking water	Dump station	Pets	Wheelchair	Recreation	Fee	Season	Can reserve	Stay limit
77	Coyote Creek SP	·	·	47		WE	F	·	·		·	·	HF	$-$$		·	14
78	El Porvenir		·	19			V		·		·		HFR	$$	May–Oct		14
79	E. V. Long		·	21	16		V		·		·		F	$$	May–Oct		14
80	McAlister Lake			D			V				·		F				14
81	Morphy Lake State Park			24	18		V				·		FB	$-$$			14
82	Storrie Lake State Park	·	·	45		WE	F	·	·	·	·	·	HFB	$-$$		·	14
83	Villanueva State Park	·	·	33		WE	F	·	·	·	·	·	HF	$-$$		·	14

Hookups: W = Water, E = Electric, S = Sewer

Toilets: F = Flush, V = Vault, P = Pit, C = Chemical

Recreation: H = Hiking, S = Swimming, F = Fishing, B = Boating, L = Boat Launch, O = Off-Highway Driving, R = Horseback Riding

Fee (per-night campsite cost): $ = $0 to $5; $$ = $6 to $10; $$$ = $11 to $20.

Maximum Trailer/RV length given in feet. Stay limit given in days. If no entry under Maximum RV length where RV sites are available, no restriction is in place.

If no entry under Season, campground is open all year. If no entry under Fee, camping is free.

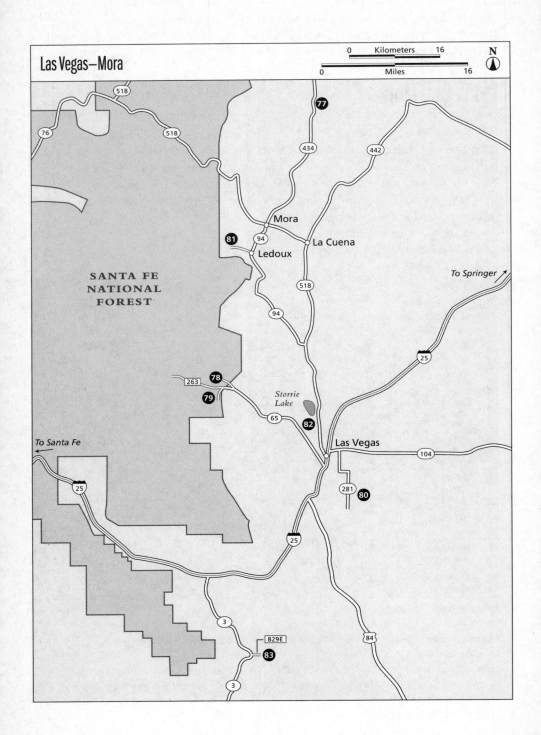

Las Vegas–Mora

0   Kilometers   16
0   Miles   16

N

518

76

518

77

434   442

Mora

81   94   La Cuena

Ledoux

SANTA FE
NATIONAL
FOREST

518

To Springer

94

25

263   78

79

Storrie
Lake

65   82

To Santa Fe

Las Vegas   104

25

281   80

25

To Santa Fe

84

3

829E

83

3

77 Coyote Creek State Park

Location: 16 miles north of Mora
GPS: N36 10.672' / W105 14.109'
Sites: 47 sites for tents and RVs
Facilities: Flush toilets, tables, grills, drinking water, visitor center, group sites, electricity, dump station, showers, playground, and hiking trails; wheelchair-accessible facilities
Fee: $ to $$, annual permit available
Elevation: 7,700 feet
Management: New Mexico State Parks Department; (575) 387-2328; www.emnrd.state.nm.us/SPD/coyotecreeklakestatepark.html
Reservations: None
Activities: Hiking and fishing
Season: Year-round
Finding the campground: From Mora travel 16 miles north on NM 434 to the campground.
About the campground: Coyote Creek is a pleasant place to camp if you enjoy viewing the mountains from a distance. It also makes a nice stopover on your way deeper into the Rockies. All the usual state park amenities are here, scattered amid a light spruce forest. Easy hiking trails lead through the forest, and fishing is excellent in Coyote Creek and the beaver ponds along it.

78 El Porvenir

Location: 16 miles northwest of Las Vegas
GPS: N35 42.619' / W105 24.734'
Sites: 19 sites for tents and RVs
Facilities: Vault toilets, tables, grills, and drinking water
Fee: $$
Elevation: 7,600 feet
Management: Santa Fe National Forest, Pecos/Las Vegas Ranger District; (505) 425-3534
Reservations: None
Activities: Hiking, fishing, and horseback riding
Season: May through October
Finding the campground: From Las Vegas travel northwest 15 miles on NM 65 to the campground. The last mile is via an unmarked dirt road that veers right off of the highway just before the El Porvenir Christian Camp.
About the campground: It's hard to find a campground on the eastern slope of the Rockies that qualifies as unpopular. And, while El Porvenir is far from unpopular, it is at least a bit less popular than spots farther into the mountains. That isn't to say that this camp is any less attractive, though. The pines are dense, and fishing is possible in Gallinas Creek. Also, the trail to Hermit's Peak is nearby.

79 E.V. Long

Location: 18 miles northwest of Las Vegas
GPS: N35 41.886' / W105 25.367'
Sites: 21 sites for tents and RVs
Facilities: Vault toilets, tables, grills, and drinking water
Fee: $$
Elevation: 7,500 feet
Management: Santa Fe National Forest, Pecos/Las Vegas Ranger District; (505) 425-3534
Reservations: None
Activities: Fishing
Season: May through October
Finding the campground: From Las Vegas travel northwest 13 miles on NM 65. Turn west onto FR 263 and go 2.1 miles. Turn south onto FR 156 and go 200 yards to the campground entrance.
About the campground: Like its neighbor El Porvenir, this camp is just a fraction less popular than many camps farther north and west, but you can still expect both of them to fill on most summer weekends. Try either of them on weekdays if you're looking for solitude.

80 McAlister Lake

Location: 7 miles southeast of Las Vegas
GPS: N35 31.361' / W105 10.164'
Sites: Dispersed
Facilities: Vault toilets
Fee: None
Elevation: 6,650 feet
Management: New Mexico Department of Game and Fish; (505) 827-7882; www.wildlife.state.nm.us
Reservations: None
Activities: Fishing
Season: Year-round
Finding the campground: From I-25 take exit 345 and travel east 1 mile on NM 104. Turn south onto NM 281 and go 7 miles to the lake.
About the campground: This New Mexico Department of Game and Fish lake is well worth the stop if you like wide-open spaces and lake fishing. The lake is stocked, and if you yearn for the smell of pines, the mountains are just a short drive away.

81 Morphy Lake State Park

Location: 11 miles southwest of Mora
GPS: N35 56.446' / W105 23.717'

Sites: 24 sites for tents and RVs
Facilities: Vault toilets, tables, and grills
Fee: $ to $$, annual permit available
Elevation: 7,800 feet
Management: New Mexico State Parks Department; (575) 387-2328; www.emnrd.state.nm.us/SPD/morphylakestatepark.html
Reservations: None
Activities: Fishing
Season: Year-round
Finding the campground: From Mora travel south 6 miles on NM 94. Turn west onto FR 635 and go 3 miles to the park.
About the campground: Morphy Lake isn't a typical state park campground. Not only does a very rough, steep road limit access, but there are no developed sites. The lake is beautiful, with a rocky shoreline surrounded by dense pines. You may actually be able to break away from the crowds at Morphy, but if you drive anything but a four-wheel drive vehicle, call ahead for road conditions.

82 Storrie Lake State Park

Location: 4 miles north of Las Vegas
GPS: N35 39.461' / W105 13.936'
Sites: 45 sites for tents and RVs
Facilities: Flush toilets, tables, grills, drinking water, visitor center, group sites, electricity, dump station, showers, and playground; wheelchair-accessible facilities
Fee: $ to $$, annual permit available
Elevation: 6,400 feet
Management: New Mexico State Parks Department; (505) 425-7278; www.emnrd.state.nm.us/SPD/storrielakestatepark.html
Reservations: Call (877) 664-7787; http://newmexicostateparks.reserveamerica.com
Activities: Hiking, fishing, boating, waterskiing, sailing, windsurfing, and scenic driving
Season: Year-round
Finding the campground: From Las Vegas travel 5 miles north on NM 518 to the campground.
About the campground: Like Las Vegas itself, Storrie Lake presents a nice gateway to the mountains. You can sit on the shore watching your line and find yourself mesmerized by the beauty of the not-too-distant peaks of the Sangre de Cristos. If a bit more activity is your style, bring a sailboard (and a wet suit) and give the breezes here a whirl.

83 Villanueva State Park

Location: 31 miles southwest of Las Vegas
GPS: N35 15.883' / W105 20.064'
Sites: 33 sites for tents and RVs

Facilities: Flush toilets, tables, grills, drinking water, visitor center, group sites, electricity, dump station, showers, playground, and hiking trails; wheelchair-accesible facilities
Fee: $ to $$, annual permit available
Elevation: 5,600 feet
Management: New Mexico State Parks Department; (575) 421-2957; www.emnrd.state.nm.us/SPD/villanuevastatepark.html
Reservations: Call (877) 664-7787; http://newmexicostateparks.reserveamerica.com
Activities: Hiking and fishing
Season: Year-round
Finding the campground: From I-25 south of Las Vegas, take exit 323 and travel south on NM 3. In the village of Villanueva, bear east on CR B29E and drive about 1 mile to the park.
About the campground: Villanueva is for lovers of the Southwest lifestyle. There are historic ruins to hike to, the campsites are designed to resemble a native village, and the whole park is situated amid red sandstone bluffs on the banks of the Pecos River. The setting is picturesque, but don't come looking for mountain scenery and pine trees.

Pecos

The mountains north of the town of Pecos have always been a popular destination, but ever-increasing numbers of campers are discovering the rugged beauty found here. The attraction lies in the easy access to the Pecos Wilderness plus the trophy-quality fishing in the Pecos River. Some campgrounds are designated as equestrian camps, and the area is especially popular with trail riders.

The region has a history in mining and draws students of geology to the red-walled canyons leading into the mountains. Amateur rock collectors also come looking for slivers of mineral treasure left behind by the miners.

Most people, though, come just for the smell of the pine trees and the whisper of the wind.

84 Field Tract

Location: 6 miles north of Pecos
GPS: N35 41.202' / W105 41.584'
Sites: 20 sites for tents and RVs
Facilities: Vault toilets, tables, grills, drinking water, and shelters
Fee: $$
Elevation: 7,400 feet
Management: Santa Fe National Forest, Pecos/Las Vegas Ranger District; (505) 757-6121
Reservations: None
Activities: Hiking and fishing
Season: May through October
Finding the campground: From Pecos travel 6 miles north on NM 63 to the campground.

Herds of deer are a common sight in the mountains across the state.
SALLY JOHNSON

		Group sites	RV sites	Total # of sites	Max. RV length	Hookups	Toilets	Showers	Drinking water	Dump station	Pets	Wheelchair	Recreation	Fee	Season	Can reserve	Stay limit
84	**Field Tract**		·	20			V		·		·		HF	$$	May–Oct		14
85	**Iron Gate**		·	14	16		V				·		HR		May–Oct		14
86	**Jack's Creek**	·	·	39	16		V		·		·		HFR	$$	May–Oct		14

Hookups: W = Water, E = Electric, S = Sewer

Toilets: F = Flush, V = Vault, P = Pit, C = Chemical

Recreation: H = Hiking, S = Swimming, F = Fishing, B = Boating, L = Boat Launch, O = Off-Highway Driving,
   R = Horseback Riding

Fee (per-night campsite cost): $ = $0 to $5; $$ = $6 to $10; $$$ = $11 to $20.

Maximum Trailer/RV length given in feet. Stay limit given in days. If no entry under Maximum RV length where RV sites are
   available, no restriction is in place.

If no entry under Season, campground is open all year. If no entry under Fee, camping is free.

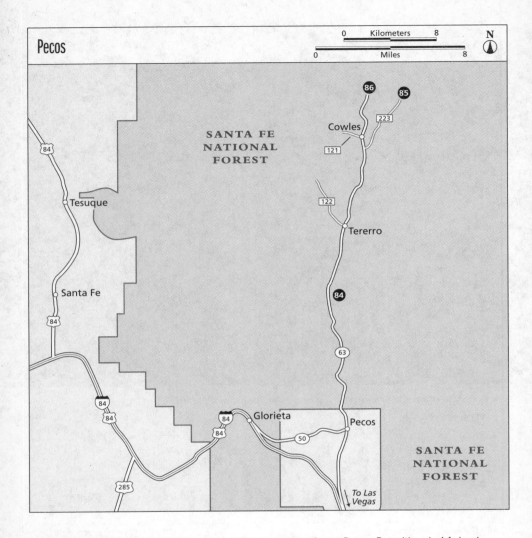

SANTA FE
NATIONAL
FOREST

About the campground: Field Tract is the elite campground near Pecos. But with only 14 developed sites plus 6 three-sided Adirondack shelters, it can be very difficult to find a spot open, even midweek. The rushing water of the Pecos River means that anglers keep this place hopping throughout the summer. The good news is that early fall camping is quite comfortable, especially if you're lucky enough to snag one of the shelters. Stone fireplaces make these sites a cozy retreat from the rest of the world even in a cold rain shower.

85 Iron Gate

Location: 19 miles north of Pecos
GPS: N35 50.397' / W105 37.219'

Sites: 14 sites for tents and RVs
Facilities: Vault toilets, tables, grills, and corral
Fee: None
Elevation: 9,400 feet
Management: Santa Fe National Forest, Pecos/Las Vegas Ranger District; (505) 757-6121
Reservations: None
Activities: Hiking and horseback riding
Season: May through October
Finding the campground: From Pecos travel 14 miles north on NM 63. Turn northeast onto FR 223 and go 4.5 miles to the campground.
About the campground: You're gonna love this camp—if you can get there. Rough roads and sheer distance keep many away, but that means more peace and quiet for you. Bring the horses because there are corrals and plenty of trails into the Pecos Wilderness. Be sure to call ahead for road conditions.

86 Jack's Creek

Location: 18.5 miles north of Pecos
GPS: N35 50.271' / W105 39.450'
Sites: 39 sites for tents and RVs
Facilities: Vault toilets, tables, grills, drinking water, and corral
Fee: $$
Elevation: 8,900 feet
Management: Santa Fe National Forest, Pecos/Las Vegas Ranger District; (505) 757-6121
Reservations: None
Activities: Hiking, fishing, and horseback riding
Season: May through October
Finding the campground: From Pecos travel 19 miles north on NM 63 to the campground.
About the campground: There's hope that sites at this very popular campground will soon be on the reservation system. Currently only the two group areas can be reserved, but keep your fingers crossed for the rest. If you're planning a trip to the Pecos area, call the National Recreation Reservation Service at (877) 444-6777 to check for the availability of reservable campsites.

If you do manage to get a site at Jack's Creek, you won't be disappointed. The campground was fully refurbished during a cleanup of potentially hazardous materials from the abandoned Terrero Mine. The benefit to campers is a large, comfortable campground. Besides fishing access to Jack's Creek, there are horse corrals and plenty of trails to explore.

Santa Rosa

Santa Rosa specializes in two things: respite for the weary traveler and cool, clear waters for recreation and thrill seekers. As a stopover along historic US Route 66, the town has its share of retro-design motels and roadside cafes. Sandwiched between these is a mix of modern chain motels and quaint Mexican food restaurants.

Gaillardia pulchella, *commonly called "Indian Blanket," add color to the desert highways of the state from May to mid-June.*

The word "oasis" is an understatement when referring to Santa Rosa—water is everywhere. Besides the Pecos River and its reservoirs, there are spring-fed ponds and natural playas. Of international renown to scuba divers is the Blue Hole, a spring-fed limestone shaft that reportedly is connected to Carlsbad Caverns, more than 200 miles away. The bottom of the shaft is now sealed with a locked grate buried beneath layers of silt, creating an 82-foot-deep tank for diving. The water is cold but crystal clear, creating near-perfect conditions for dive training. A stop by Blue Hole is a nice diversion even for non-divers.

87 Santa Rosa Lake State Park

Location: 7 miles north of Santa Rosa
GPS: N35 01.705' / W104 40.965'
Sites: 75 sites for tents and RVs
Facilities: Flush toilets, tables, grills, drinking water, visitor center, group sites, electricity, dump station, showers, and hiking trails; wheelchair-accessible facilities
Fee: $ to $$, annual permit available
Elevation: 4,800 feet
Management: New Mexico State Parks Department; (575) 472-3110; www.emnrd.state.nm.us/SPD/santarosastatelakestatepark.html

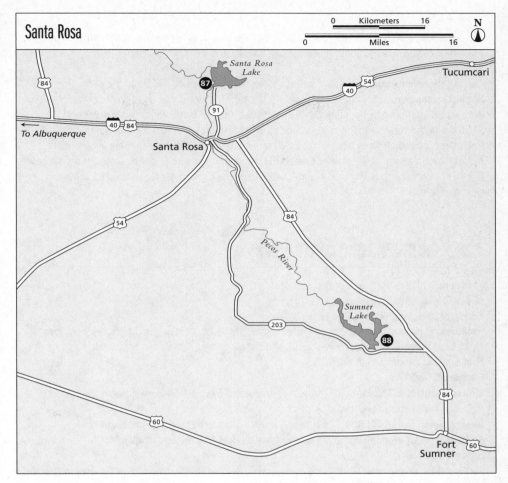

0 Kilometers 16
0 Miles 16

N

To Albuquerque

Tucumcari

Santa Rosa Lake

Santa Rosa

Pecos River

Sumner Lake

Fort Sumner

		Group sites	RV sites	Total # of sites	Max. RV length	Hookups	Toilets	Showers	Drinking water	Dump station	Pets	Wheelchair	Recreation	Fee	Season	Can reserve	Stay limit
87	Santa Rosa Lake State Park	·	·	75		WE	F	·	·	·	·		HFB	$–$$		·	14
88	Sumner Lake State Park	·	·	50		WE	FV	·	·	·	·		HFB	$–$$		·	14

Hookups: W = Water, E = Electric, S = Sewer

Toilets: F = Flush, V = Vault, P = Pit, C = Chemical

Recreation: H = Hiking, S = Swimming, F = Fishing, B = Boating, L = Boat Launch, O = Off-Highway Driving,
   R = Horseback Riding

Fee (per-night campsite cost): $ = $0 to $5; $$ = $6 to $10; $$$ = $11 to $20.

Maximum Trailer/RV length given in feet. Stay limit given in days. If no entry under Maximum RV length where RV sites are
   available, no restriction is in place.

If no entry under Season, campground is open all year. If no entry under Fee, camping is free.

Reservations: Call (877) 664-7787; http://newmexicostateparks.reserveamerica.com
Activities: Hiking, fishing, boating, waterskiing, sailing, and windsurfing
Season: Year-round
Finding the campground: From Santa Rosa travel north 8 miles on NM 91 to the park.
About the campground: Santa Rosa Lake is a US Army Corps of Engineers lake, but the campgrounds are managed by the state parks department. Federal recreation passports are not accepted in the state park. The campgrounds are set high on a bluff overlooking Santa Rosa Lake and offer outstanding views. You can enjoy all of the same activities here that are available at any of New Mexico's premier water sports lakes, but with surprisingly fewer people. The campgrounds are well designed with plenty of space per site and all the usual amenities, including some sites with electricity.

88 Sumner Lake State Park

Location: 16 miles northwest of Fort Sumner
GPS: N34 36.252' / W104 22.602'
Sites: 50 sites for tents and RVs
Facilities: Flush and vault toilets, tables, grills, shelters, visitor center, group sites, showers, electricity, boat ramps and dock, dump station, and drinking water; wheelchair-accessible facilities
Fee: $ to $$, annual permit available
Elevation: 4,300 feet
Management: New Mexico State Parks Department; (575) 355-2541; www.emnrd.state.nm.us/SPD/sumnerlakestatepark.html
Reservations: Call (877) 664-7787; http://newmexicostateparks.reserveamerica.com
Activities: Hiking, swimming, fishing, boating, waterskiing, sailing, and windsurfing
Season: Year-round
Finding the campground: From Fort Sumner travel north on US 84 about 16 miles. Turn west onto New Mexico Highway 203 and go 6 miles to the campground.
About the campground: Tucked away in the Pecos River Valley south of Santa Rosa, this quiet lake is not heavily used, yet. With the numbers of water sports enthusiasts exploding yearly, they are bound to find Fort Sumner sooner or later.

There are four named campgrounds at Sumner Lake: East River, West River, East Side, and Main. East Side and Main offer lake access. Both of these include some sites with electricity, but only Main has comfort stations with flush toilets and showers. Sites are set amid juniper and mesquite, but shelters provide shade. Besides offering easy access to the lakeshore, these two campgrounds have views of the lake.

The river campgrounds—East River and West River—are on the back side of the dam, making them a quieter choice. River use is restricted to fishing only; no wading or floating is allowed. These sites are primitive but pleasant. In addition to the metal shelters, there are some shade trees along the river.

Southwest

Loneliness here permeates even the air. Much of this corner of the state has the hushed feel of a ghost town. People are thinly scattered across the deserts and mountains, and though they welcome visitors, many choose to live here because the solitude suits them.

Activities in the region range from rock collecting at long-forgotten mines to rock climbing in the Gila National Forest. You can fish the largest reservoirs in the state or crawl through ancient cliff dwellings. Just beware—the quiet of this place is addicting.

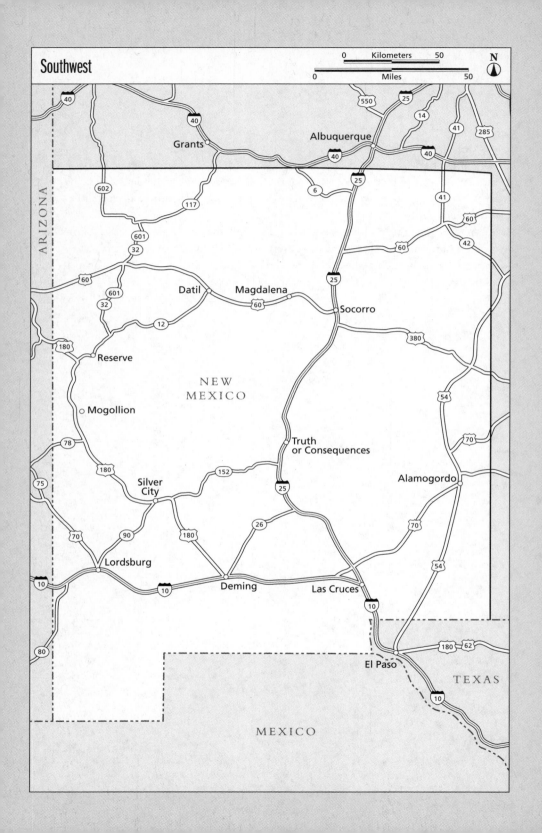

Socorro-Datil

If your fondest desire is to be alone, this stretch of desert dotted with green mountains is a good place to end up. It wasn't always that way. Half a century ago the area was a booming mining community. Today Socorro is home to the New Mexico Tech School of Mines. Farther west you'll find one of the most lonely but interesting places in the country: the National Radio Astronomy Observatory Very Large Array Telescope (VLA). Using an array of twenty-seven radio antennas (picture giant satellite dishes), scientists here map the universe by capturing sound waves emitted by objects in space. Parts of the Jodie Foster movie *Contact* were filmed here, though the concept of "listening" to space in the movie was dramatized somewhat. Both the VLA and the School of Mines offer tours.

The Magdalena area was once a bustling mining community where fortunes were made and lost in the search for lead, copper, and even silver. Of interest to rock and mineral collectors are the abandoned mines, which allow collecting at their dump sites. Prize samples of vivid blue azurite, turquoise smithsonite, and green malachite can be found if you're willing to pay a collecting fee and spend a few hours sifting through the mine dumps.

For more information:
National Radio Astronomy Observatory VLA
GPS: N34 04.379' / W107 37.386'
www.vla.nrao.edu

Magdalena Chamber of Commerce
902 W. First St.
Magdalena, NM 87825
(866) 854-3217
www.magdalena-nm.com

Socorro County Chamber of Commerce
101 Plaza St.
Socorro, NM 87801
(575) 835-0424
www.socorrochamber.org

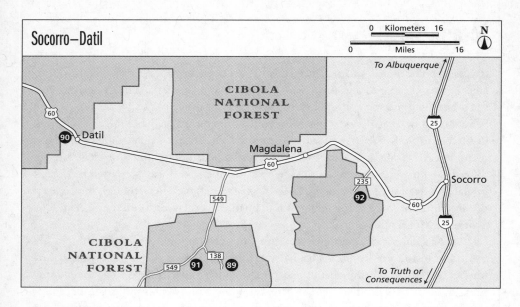

		Group sites	RV sites	Total # of sites	Max. RV length	Hookups	Toilets	Showers	Drinking water	Dump station	Pets	Wheelchair	Recreation	Fee	Season	Can reserve	Stay limit
89	**Bear Trap**			4	20		V				·		HO		May–Oct		14
90	**Datil Well**		·	22			V		·		·		H	$			14
91	**Hughes Mill**			2	20		V				·		HO		May–Oct		14
92	**Water Canyon**		·	4	22		V				·		HO		May–Oct		14

Hookups: W = Water,   E = Electric,   S = Sewer

Toilets: F = Flush,   V = Vault,   P = Pit,   C = Chemical

Recreation: H = Hiking,   S = Swimming,   F = Fishing,   B = Boating,   L = Boat Launch,   O = Off-Highway Driving,
   R = Horseback Riding

Fee (per-night campsite cost): $ = $0 to $5; $$ = $6 to $10; $$$ = $11 to $20.

Maximum Trailer/RV length given in feet. Stay limit given in days. If no entry under Maximum RV length where RV sites are
   available, no restriction is in place.

If no entry under Season, campground is open all year. If no entry under Fee, camping is free.

89 Bear Trap

Location: 30 miles southwest of Magdalena
GPS: N33 52.980' / W107 30.846'
Sites: 4 sites for tents
Facilities: Vault toilets, tables, and grills
Fee: None
Elevation: 8,500 feet
Management: Cibola National Forest, Magdalena Ranger District; (575) 854-2381
Reservations: None
Activities: Hiking and four-wheel driving
Season: May through October
Finding the campground: From Magdalena travel west 15 miles on US 60. Turn south onto FR 549 and go 12 miles.
About the campground: By the time you get to this isolated campground, you may be wondering why they didn't call it "Camper Trap" instead. It is a very long and bumpy road to the campground, but at the end of the journey, you'll find four quiet, streamside primitive sites that you can call home. You may encounter a few fellow travelers, but it's not likely.

90 Datil Well

Location: Datil
GPS: N34 09.254' / W107 51.493'
Sites: 22 sites for tents and RVs
Facilities: Vault toilets, tables, grills, and drinking water
Fee: $
Elevation: 7,400 feet
Management: Bureau of Land Management, Socorro Field Office; (575) 835-0412; www.blm.gov/nm
Reservations: None
Activities: Hiking
Season: Year-round
Finding the campground: In Datil travel west on US 60 to the campground (just past mile marker 77).
About the campground: This is a lovely spot to spend a night or two during your journey through southwest New Mexico. The sites are well spaced among low-growing piñon and juniper trees, with some very large pull-through sites for big RV rigs.

91 Hughes Mill

Location: 30 miles southwest of Magdalena
GPS: N33 51.411' / W107 32.526'

The radio telescopes at the VLA site stretch skyward from the desert floor.

Sites: 2 sites for tents
Facilities: Vault toilets, tables, and grills
Fee: None
Elevation: 8,100 feet
Management: Cibola National Forest, Magdalena Ranger District; (575) 854-2381
Reservations: None
Activities: Hiking and four-wheel driving
Season: May through October
Finding the campground: From Magdalena travel west 15 miles on US 60. Turn south onto FR 549 and go 15 miles to the campground.
About the campground: As with neighboring Bear Trap, the object of this game is just getting to the campground. If you can handle the long, rough road, then you deserve the quiet camp at the end of the journey. The trailhead for Mt. Withington Lookout is here, which makes it a bit more likely that you will encounter fellow humans, but you could just as easily have the place to yourself.

92 Water Canyon

Location: 19 miles southwest of Socorro
GPS: N34 01.454' / W107 07.819'
Sites: 4 sites for tents and RVs
Facilities: Vault toilets, tables, and grills
Fee: None
Elevation: 6,800 feet
Management: Cibola National Forest, Magdalena Ranger District; (575) 854-2381
Reservations: None
Activities: Hiking, four-wheel driving, rock collecting, and mountain biking
Season: May through October
Finding the campground: From Socorro travel west 13 miles on US 60. Turn south onto FR 235 and go 6 miles to the campground.
About the campground: Don't come to this part of the state looking for deluxe remodeled campgrounds. Just come looking for quiet places to enjoy the outdoors. From Water Canyon you can drive, hike, bike, or climb to your heart's content with the Magdalena Mountains at your doorstep via trails and long-forgotten mining roads.

Reserve-Mogollon

These two communities are located in Catron County, which boasts the lowest population per square mile of any county in the state. Believe it or not, even the campgrounds aren't crowded. Don't come here looking for the touristy side of New Mexico; there's probably not a Mexican-food restaurant in the whole county.

What you will find is beautiful country and miles of poorly maintained roads to explore. Bring a fishing pole and a good book, and plan to stay a while. It also

Collecting rocks and minerals at the abandoned mines is one form of recreation for campers at Water Canyon.

wouldn't hurt to bring a winch in case you get stuck, because it will be a long wait for help in this county.

Reserve is the best place in the county to buy forgotten supplies or fuel. Mogollon, on the other hand, is more of a living museum than anything else. Located at the end of perhaps the state's narrowest, most winding paved road, it presents a colorful portrait of a mining past that still lives. Heed all warning signs concerning road conditions, or you'll need that winch.

		Group sites	RV sites	Total # of sites	Max. RV length	Hookups	Toilets	Showers	Drinking water	Dump station	Pets	Wheelchair	Recreation	Fee	Season	Can reserve	Stay limit
93	Apache Creek		•	20			V				•		HF				14
94	Gilita		•	6	17		V				•		HF		May–Nov		14
95	Head of the Ditch		•	2	30		V				•		HFR		Apr–Nov		14
96	Pueblo Park			7			V				•		H		May–Nov		14
97	Quemado Lake RA		•	62	30	E	V		•		•	•	FB	$$	Apr–Nov		14
98	Dipping Vat		•	40			V		•		•	•	HF	$	Apr–Nov		14
99	Willow Creek			6			V				•		HF	$$	Apr–Nov		14

Hookups: W = Water,   E = Electric,   S = Sewer
Toilets: F = Flush,   V = Vault,   P = Pit,   C = Chemical
Recreation: H = Hiking,   S = Swimming,   F = Fishing,   B = Boating,   L = Boat Launch,   O = Off-Highway Driving,
    R = Horseback Riding
Fee (per-night campsite cost): $ = $0 to $5; $$ = $6 to $10; $$$ = $11 to $20.
Maximum Trailer/RV length given in feet. Stay limit given in days. If no entry under Maximum RV length where RV sites are
    available, no restriction is in place.
If no entry under Season, campground is open all year. If no entry under Fee, camping is free.

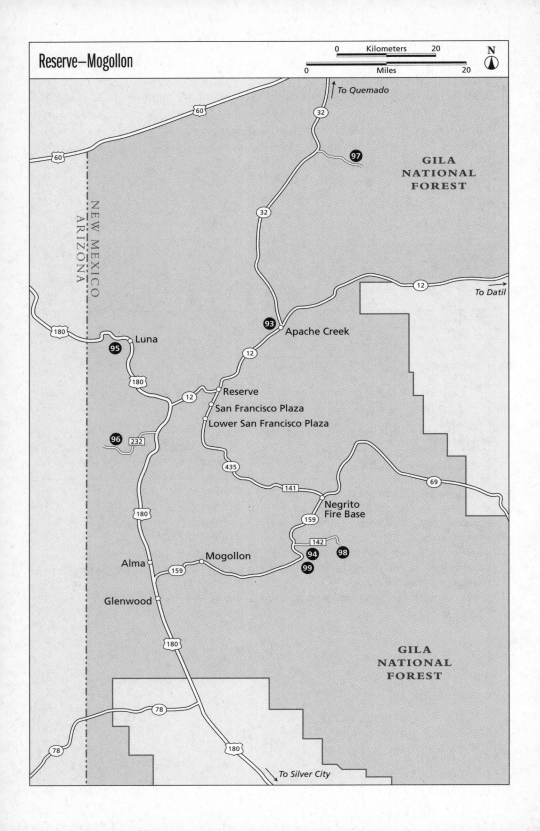

93 Apache Creek

Location: 12 miles north of Reserve
GPS: N33 49.712' / W108 37.678'
Sites: 20 sites for tents and RVs
Facilities: Vault toilets, tables, and grills
Fee: None
Elevation: 6,400 feet
Management: Gila National Forest, Reserve Ranger District; (575) 533-6232
Reservations: None
Activities: Hiking and fishing
Season: Year-round
Finding the campground: From Reserve travel northeast on NM 12 about 11 miles to the campground.
About the campground: Trees, shade, and a nearby river make this another of the hidden gems tucked away in the Gila. It presents a picturesque spot from which to base your explorations of the southwestern portions of the state, including the Gila Wilderness.

94 Gilita

Location: 32 miles east of Alma
GPS: N33 24.623' / W108 34.820'
Sites: 6 sites for tents and RVs
Facilities: Vault toilets, tables, and grills
Fee: None
Elevation: 7,100 feet
Management: Gila National Forest, Reserve Ranger District; (575) 533-6232
Reservations: None
Activities: Hiking and fishing
Season: May through November
Finding the campground: From US 180 south of Alma, turn east onto NM 159. Travel east 17 miles to Mogollon and then another 17 miles to the campground.
About the campground: If it's hard for you to believe that a campground in the woods at such a mild elevation wouldn't be a busy spot, you haven't been to this part of the state. The crowds are not here. Just peaceful pines and six streamside sites.

95 Head of the Ditch

Location: 2 miles west of Luna
GPS: N33 49.009' / W108 59.237'

Sites: 2 sites for tents and RVs
Facilities: Vault toilets
Fee: None
Elevation: 7,100 feet
Management: Gila National Forest, Luna Work Station; (575) 547-2612
Reservations: None
Activities: Hiking, fishing, horseback riding, and rock collecting
Season: April through November
Finding the campground: From Luna travel 2 miles west on US 180 to the campground entrance.
About the campground: You aren't in Arizona yet, but you can see it from the top of the hill. This tiny camp offers what few places in the state can offer: beautiful agates and even quartz geodes for those willing to search for them. The campground is usually empty of overnight visitors, but rockhounds from across the country often pass through here in search of mineral treasure. Fishing in the San Francisco River isn't a bad way to pass the time either.

96 Pueblo Park

Location: 18 miles southwest of Reserve
GPS: N33 35.603' / W108 57.687'
Sites: 7 sites for tents
Facilities: Vault toilets, tables, and grills
Fee: None
Elevation: 7,000 feet
Management: Gila National Forest, Reserve Ranger District; (575) 533-6232
Reservations: None
Activities: Hiking and rock collecting
Season: May through November
Finding the campground: From Reserve travel 7.5 miles west on NM 12 to the junction with US 180. Turn south and go 6 miles. Turn west onto FR 232 and go 6.5 miles to the campground.
About the campground: If you haven't figured it out yet, this area of the state is rich with mineral treasures that draw numerous rock collectors. This camp is no exception. Other than the rockhounds and the occasional hiker, Pueblo Park sees little use. It is a beautiful spot from which to enjoy the rugged scenery.

97 Quemado Lake Recreation Area

Location: 23 miles south of Quemado
GPS: N34 08.276' / W108 29.495'
Sites: 62 sites for tents and RVs
Facilities: Vault toilets, tables, grills, electricity, and drinking water; wheelchair-accessible facilities
Fee: $$
Elevation: 7,800 feet

Management: Gila National Forest, Quemado Ranger District; (575) 773-4678
Reservations: None
Activities: Fishing and boating
Season: April through November
Finding the campground: In Quemado travel south on NM 32 and go 13.9 miles to FR 103. Turn east and follow the signs to the campgrounds.
About the campground: This is the most developed recreational area in the entire region. Two campgrounds overlook the 130-acre lake. Juniper is the larger, with 36 sites, including 18 electric hookup sites. The electricity comes at the price of closeness to your neighbors, but the extra convenience is nice. Piñon campground has 22 additional sites suitable for tents or small trailers. Both campgrounds are modern and well maintained.

Fishing this lake is best accomplished by boat, but only electric motors are allowed. Even though it is the only place you're likely to find a crowd in all of Catron County, it's a pretty spot and easily accessed.

98 Dipping Vat

Location: 50 miles southeast of Reserve
GPS: N33 25.354' / W108 30.037'
Sites: 40 sites for tents and RVs
Facilities: Vault toilets, tables, and grills
Fee: $
Elevation: 7,300 feet
Management: Gila National Forest, Reserve Ranger District; (575) 533-6232
Reservations: None
Activities: Hiking and fishing
Season: April through November
Finding the campground: From Reserve travel 44 miles south on NM 435 (which becomes FR 141). Turn east onto FR 142 and go another 6 miles to the campground.
About the campground: There are two kinds of campers in this world, and you can usually tell the difference by the amount of road dust on the outside (and the inside) of their vehicles. If you're the dusty type who will travel any road if there's a promise of a great camping spot, then Snow Lake is for you. The campground is in a light pine forest perched on a hill overlooking the pretty lake. Over all, it's a nice place to camp if you can handle the road.

99 Willow Creek

Location: 31 miles east of Alma
GPS: N33 24.098' / W108 34.870'
Sites: 6 sites for tents
Facilities: Vault toilets, tables, and grills
Fee: $$

Idyllic campsites with views of the water are the standard at Snow Lake.

Elevation: 8,000 feet
Management: Gila National Forest, Reserve Ranger District; (575) 533-6232
Reservations: None
Activities: Fishing and hiking
Season: April through November
Finding the campground: From US 180 south of Alma, turn east onto NM 159. Travel east 17 miles to Mogollon and then another 16 miles to the campground.
About the campground: "Quiet" and "secluded" are the best words to describe this appropriately named camp. All of the six sites have access to Willow Creek, and trails into the Gila Wilderness are a short distance away.

Truth or Consequences

Truth or Consequences bills itself as a southwestern recreation paradise. While that may be a bit of an exaggeration, the area does have the big advantage of being sandwiched between two of the state's most popular water sports lakes. The scenery is pure Southwest: red bluffs and cactus, with a faint blue line of mountains on the distant horizon.

In their rush to get to the lakes, many people often overlook the fun things to do in town. Before the name changed to the distinctive "T or C," the town was called Hot Springs. The historic bathhouse and spa district, where you can soak away your cares in the healing mineral waters, is located downtown. It makes a nice break from all the activity at the lake campgrounds.

Another diversion away from the state parks is rock collecting. As with many areas of the state, rockhounds come here looking for unusual finds. In the Caballo Mountains the treasure includes carnelian, a vivid orange agate that polishes into exquisite jewelry.

For more information:
Truth or Consequences & Sierra County Chamber of Commerce
207 S. Foch St.
Truth or Consequences, NM 87901
(575) 894-3536 or www.torcchamber.com

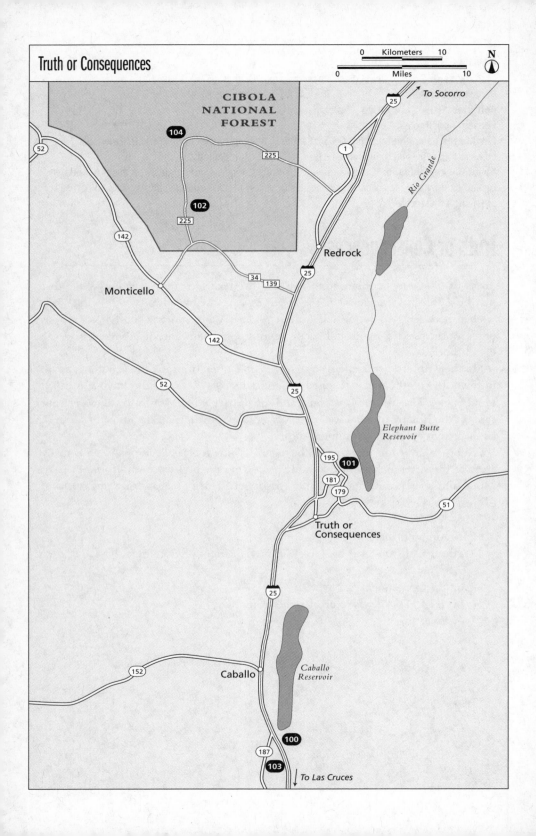

Truth or Consequences

		Group sites	RV sites	Total # of sites	Max. RV length	Hookups	Toilets	Showers	Drinking water	Dump station	Pets	Wheelchair	Recreation	Fee	Season	Can reserve	Stay limit
100	Caballo Lake State Park	•	•	170		WE	F	•	•	•	•		HFBL	$-$$		•	14
101	Elephant Butte Lake State Park	•	•	144		WE	F	•	•	•	•	•	HFBL	$-$$		•	14
102	Luna Park			3			V				•		HR		Apr-Nov		14
103	Percha Dam State Park	•		50		WE	F	•	•		•		HF	$-$$		•	14
104	Springtime			6			V				•		HO	$	May-Oct		14

Hookups: W = Water, E = Electric, S = Sewer
Toilets: F = Flush, V = Vault, P = Pit, C = Chemical
Recreation: H = Hiking, S = Swimming, F = Fishing, B = Boating, L = Boat Launch, O = Off-Highway Driving,
   R = Horseback Riding
Fee (per-night campsite cost): $ = $0 to $5; $$ = $6 to $10; $$$ = $11 to $20.
Maximum Trailer/RV length given in feet. Stay limit given in days. If no entry under Maximum RV length where RV sites are
   available, no restriction is in place.
If no entry under Season, campground is open all year. If no entry under Fee, camping is free.

100 Caballo Lake State Park

Location: 16 miles south of Truth or Consequences
GPS: N32 54.442' / W107 18.615'
Sites: 170 sites for tents and RVs
Facilities: Flush toilets, tables, grills, drinking water, visitor center, group sites, electricity, dump station, showers, marina, playground, and hiking trails
Fee: $ to $$, annual permit available
Elevation: 4,100 feet
Management: New Mexico State Parks Department; (575) 743-3942; www.emnrd.state.nm.us/SPD/caballolakestatepark.html
Reservations: Call (877) 664-7787; http://newmexicostateparks.reserveamerica.com
Activities: Hiking, fishing, boating, waterskiing, sailing, and windsurfing
Season: Year-round
Finding the campground: From I-25 south of Truth or Consequences, take exit 59 and follow the signs east to the park.
About the campground: The 170 sites here are spread among five campgrounds, four near the lake and one on the river behind the dam. If being on the lake isn't a higher priority, the riverside camp is the prettiest. There are more trees at this camp, and the rush of the water adds to the atmosphere.

If the fish aren't biting, the primitive roads on the east side of the lake lead to hours of exploration in the hills.

101 Elephant Butte Lake State Park

Location: 5 miles north of Truth or Consequences
GPS: N33 10.927' / W107 12.644'
Sites: 144 sites for tents and RVs
Facilities: Flush toilets, tables, grills, drinking water, visitor center, group sites, electricity, dump station, showers, playground, marina, and hiking trails; wheelchair-accessible facilities
Fee: $ to $$, annual permit available
Elevation: 4,500 feet
Management: New Mexico State Parks Department; (575) 744-5421; www.emnrd.state.nm.us/SPD/elephantbuttelakestatepark.html
Reservations: Call (877) 664-7787; http://newmexicostateparks.reserveamerica.com
Activities: Hiking, fishing, boating, waterskiing, sailing, and windsurfing
Season: Year-round
Finding the campground: From Truth or Consequences travel 3 miles east on NM 51. Turn north on NM 179 and follow the signs to the park.
About the campground: This state park is reportedly the third-most-popular spot in the state on Memorial Day weekend. So, quite simply, don't go there, or at least not on that weekend. Other summer weekends may not be much better, but spring and fall are delightful. The campgrounds are not usually full to capacity, and the temperature isn't unbearable.

The park offers plenty of diversion away from the water, including playgrounds and nature trails.

102 Luna Park

Location: 8 miles northeast of Monticello
GPS: N33 29.754' / W107 24.919'
Sites: 3 sites for tents
Facilities: Vault toilets
Fee: None
Elevation: 7,400 feet
Management: Cibola National Forest, Magdalena Ranger District; (575) 854-2381
Reservations: None
Activities: Hiking and horseback riding
Season: April through November
Finding the campground: From Monticello travel north 5 miles on FR 135/CR 34. Turn north onto FR 225 and go 3 miles to the campground.
About the campground: This is a campground for lovers of off-road camping. The road into the campground is four-wheel drive only. The three spaces are situated amid lava beds at the foot of the San Mateo Mountains. It's hard to get here, but you'll likely have the place to yourself. Just don't come here looking for shade and bubbling brooks.

103 Percha Dam State Park

Location: 21 miles south of Truth or Consequences
GPS: N32 52.062' / W107 18.184'
Sites: 50 sites for tents and RVs
Facilities: Flush toilets, tables, grills, drinking water, group sites, electricity, showers, and playground
Fee: $ to $$, annual permit available
Elevation: 4,100 feet
Management: New Mexico State Parks Department; (575) 743-3942; www.emnrd.state.nm.us/SPD/perchadamstatepark.html
Reservations: Call (877) 664-7787; http://newmexicostateparks.reserveamerica.com
Activities: Hiking and fishing
Season: Year-round
Finding the campground: From I-25 south of Truth or Consequences, take exit 59 and follow the signs west to the park.
About the campground: Set amid towering cottonwoods, this unique state park offers a wonderful chance to hike and camp along the Rio Grande. Not usually as crowded as the two lakes to the north, Percha may be just the place for a bit of quiet contemplation.

104 Springtime

Location: 39 miles northwest of Truth or Consequences
GPS: N33 34.521' / W107 24.269'
Sites: 6 sites for tents
Facilities: Vault toilets
Fee: $
Elevation: 7,400 feet
Management: Cibola National Forest, Magdalena Ranger District; (575) 854-2381
Reservations: None
Activities: Hiking and four-wheel driving
Season: May through October
Finding the campground: From I-25 north of Truth or Consequences, take exit 100. Turn north onto NM 1 and go 4 miles. Turn west onto FR 225 and go 12 miles to the campground.
About the campground: Ranked as one of the "Top 50 Campgrounds in New Mexico" by Great Outdoors.com, Springtime is the only access camp near the Apache Kidd Wilderness. Hiking trails are near the camp. All six sites have Adirondack shelters, making this a comfortable place to camp even without a trailer (which cannot make the trip). The shelters are created so that a tent is not necessary; just bring a couple of tarps to stretch across the open side, and you'll have a cozy retreat.

The road is limited to high-clearance vehicles only. It would be wise to call ahead for specific road conditions.

Silver City-Gila Wilderness

Silver City is aptly named. When you discover it, you feel like you've found the state's hidden treasure. There are dozens of things to do here, ranging from tours of the huge copper mines to hiking in the Gila. Try stopping for a drink at a real Western saloon at Piños Altos or visit the Billy the Kid jail site. The people here love to tell about the city's history, and visitors are welcomed with open arms.

The Gila National Forest (locally shortened to "the Gila") is home to the first official wilderness area in the nation. The Gila Wilderness was created in 1924 to protect and preserve the incredible beauty found here. Once you've experienced the Gila, you'll agree it is an awe-inspiring national treasure.

For more information:
Silver City–Grant County Chamber of Commerce
3130 Hwy. 180 E., Ste. C
Silver City, NM 88061
(575) 538-3785 or (800) 548-9378
www.silvercity.org

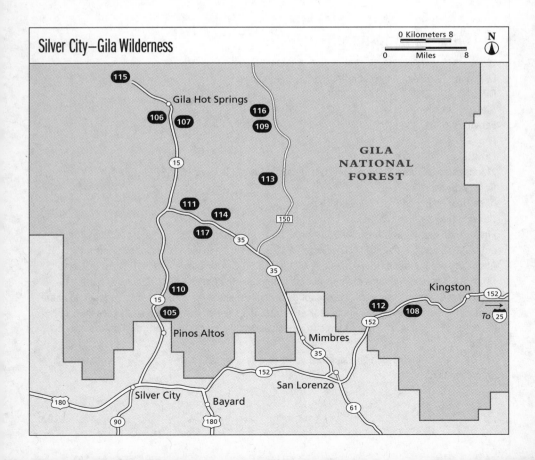

		Group sites	RV sites	Total # of sites	Max. RV length	Hookups	Toilets	Showers	Drinking water	Dump station	Pets	Wheelchair	Recreation	Fee	Season	Can reserve	Stay limit
105	Cherry Creek			12			V				•		H	$$	May-Oct		14
106	Forks		•	D			V				•		HF	$	May-Oct		14
107	Grapevine		•	D			V				•		HF	$	May-Oct		14
108	Iron Creek		•	15	17		V				•		HF	$	May-Oct		14
109	Lower Black Canyon		•	3	17		V				•		H	$	May-Oct		14
110	McMillan			3			V				•		H	$	May-Oct		14
111	Mesa		•	24			V		•		•		HFB	$$	May-Oct		14
112	Railroad Canyon			D			V				•		H		May-Oct		14
113	Rocky Canyon		•	2	17		V				•		H		May-Oct		14
114	Sapillo/ Lake Roberts	•	•	10			V				•		HFR				14
115	Scorpion		•	10	17		V		•		•		HF		May-Oct		14
116	Upper Black Canyon		•	2	22		V		•		•		HF	$	May-Oct		14
117	Upper End		•	10			V		•		•		HFB	$	May-Oct		14

Hookups: W = Water, E = Electric, S = Sewer

Toilets: F = Flush, V = Vault, P = Pit, C = Chemical

Recreation: H = Hiking, S = Swimming, F = Fishing, B = Boating, L = Boat Launch, O = Off-Highway Driving,
  R = Horseback Riding

Fee (per-night campsite cost): $ = $0 to $5; $$ = $6 to $10; $$$ = $11 to $20.

Maximum Trailer/RV length given in feet. Stay limit given in days. If no entry under Maximum RV length where RV sites are
  available, no restriction is in place.

If no entry under Season, campground is open all year. If no entry under Fee, camping is free.

105 Cherry Creek

Location: 9 miles northeast of Silver City
GPS: N32 54.854' / W108 13.453'
Sites: 12 sites for tents
Facilities: Vault toilets, tables, and grills
Fee: $$
Elevation: 6,800 feet
Management: Gila National Forest, Silver City Ranger District; (575) 388-8201

A short hike leads to the well-preserved cliff dwellings.

Reservations: None
Activities: Hiking
Season: May through October
Finding the campground: From Silver City travel 9 miles north on NM 15 to the campground.
About the campground: Cherry Creek is a nice stopover on your way deeper into the Gila. The sites are in a light pine forest next to Cherry Creek, which is fishable during spring thaw.

106 Forks

Location: 1 mile south of Gila Hot Springs
GPS: N33 11.009' / W108 12.385'
Sites: Dispersed
Facilities: Vault toilets
Fee: $
Elevation: 5,700 feet
Management: Gila National Forest, Wilderness Ranger District; (575) 536-2250
Reservations: None
Activities: Hiking and fishing
Season: May through October
Finding the campground: From Gila Hot Springs travel south 1 mile on NM 15 to the campground.
About the campground: Forks is situated at the junction of the three forks of the Gila River. The campsites are scattered among cottonwoods and low shrubs, with easy access to the rushing waters of the river. From here it's easy to see the attraction for the ancient people who called the Gila Valley their home.

107 Grapevine

Location: 2 miles south of Gila Hot Springs
GPS: N33 10.735' / W108 12.280'
Sites: Dispersed
Facilities: Vault toilets
Fee: $
Elevation: 5,700 feet
Management: Gila National Forest, Wilderness Ranger District; (575) 536-2250
Reservations: None
Activities: Hiking, fishing, and rock collecting
Season: May through October
Finding the campground: From Gila Hot Springs travel south 2 miles on NM 15 to the campground.
About the campground: Like the neighboring Forks campground, the sites here are scattered along the three forks of the Gila River. The valley is thick with cottonwood trees, providing plenty of shade from the summer sun. Camp here to fully appreciate the quiet of the Gila.

The ancestors of the Pueblo people built and lived in these cliff dwellings more than 700 years ago.

108 Iron Creek

Location: 10 miles west of Kingston
GPS: N32 54.532' / W107 48.352'
Sites: 15 sites for tents and RVs
Facilities: Vault toilets, tables, and grills
Fee: $
Elevation: 7,300 feet
Management: Gila National Forest, Wilderness Ranger District; (575) 536-2250
Reservations: None
Activities: Hiking, fishing, and rock collecting
Season: May through October
Finding the campground: From Kingston travel 10 miles west on NM 152 to the campground.
About the campground: The mere name of this campground evokes visions of miners laboring away trying to find that one streak of precious mineral hidden amid the slag. The creek is tiny but adds to the quiet atmosphere of this valley. Hiking trails lead from here into the Aldo Leopold Wilderness.

109 Lower Black Canyon

Location: 25 miles north of Mimbres
GPS: N33 10.954' / W108 02.086'
Sites: 3 sites for tents and RVs
Facilities: Vault toilets
Fee: $
Elevation: 7,200 feet
Management: Gila National Forest, Wilderness Ranger District; (575) 536-2250
Reservations: None
Activities: Hiking
Season: May through October
Finding the campground: From Mimbres travel 10 miles northwest on NM 35. Turn north onto FR 150 and go 13.5 miles to the campground road. Turn west and go through Upper Black Canyon to reach the lower sites.
About the campground: These three primitive sites are the next best things to off-road camping you'll find in the Gila without lugging a backpack. Here you can escape the crowds below and enjoy the wildness of the place.

110 McMillan

Location: 11 miles northeast of Silver City
GPS: N32 55.438' / W108 12.820'

Campsites line the forks of the Gila River at the campgrounds near the cliff dwellings.

Sites: 3 sites for tents
Facilities: Vault toilets
Fee: $
Elevation: 6,800 feet
Management: Gila National Forest, Silver City Ranger District; (575) 388-8201
Reservations: None
Activities: Hiking
Season: May through October
Finding the campground: From Silver City travel 9 miles north on NM 15 to the campground.
About the campground: Like nearby Cherry Creek, McMillan makes a good place to begin or end your journey into the Gila. Consider this camp for a first night if you will be arriving after dark. The narrow, steep roads in the Gila aren't the best place to test either your brakes or your night vision.

111 Mesa

Location: 23 miles northeast of Silver City
GPS: N33 02.170' / W108 09.326'
Sites: 24 sites for tents and RVs
Facilities: Vault toilets, tables, grills, and drinking water
Fee: $$
Elevation: 6,100 feet
Management: Gila National Forest, Wilderness Ranger District; (575) 536-2250
Reservations: None
Activities: Hiking, fishing, and boating
Season: May through October
Finding the campground: From Silver City travel 20 miles north on NM 15 and then 3 miles east on NM 35 to the campground.
About the campground: Located on the shores of Lake Roberts, this camp is probably the most popular in the Gila National Forest. Pine trees tower over the campsites, and the 72-acre lake makes a beautiful backdrop. Plan to spend some time here.

112 Railroad Canyon

Location: 10 miles west of Kingston
GPS: N32 54.447' / W107 49.016'
Sites: Dispersed
Facilities: Vault toilets
Fee: None
Elevation: 7,300 feet
Management: Gila National Forest, Wilderness Ranger District; (575) 536-2250
Reservations: None
Activities: Hiking

Season: May through October

Finding the campground: From Kingston travel 10 miles west on NM 152 to the campground.

About the campground: Primitive sites here absorb the overflow from the Iron Creek camp. You may simply prefer the wider spacing of the primitive sites. The minerals in the mine dumps and the hiking in the Aldo Leopold Wilderness are the main attractions here.

113 Rocky Canyon

Location: 19 miles north of Mimbres
GPS: N33 06.004' / W108 00.769'
Sites: 2 sites for tents and RVs
Facilities: Vault toilets
Fee: None
Elevation: 8,400 feet
Management: Gila National Forest, Wilderness Ranger District; (575) 536-2250
Reservations: None
Activities: Hiking
Season: May through October
Finding the campground: From Mimbres travel 10 miles northwest on NM 35. Turn north onto FR 150 and go 9 miles to the campground.
About the campground: If you came to the Gila to get away from traffic noise and other people, try this tiny camp. The pines and oaks protect you from the summer sun, and the peacefulness of the Gila shields you from the world.

114 Sapillo/Lake Roberts

Location: 25 miles northeast of Silver City
GPS: N33 00.634' / W108 06.871'
Sites: 10 sites for tents and RVs
Facilities: Vault toilets, tables, and grills
Fee: None
Elevation: 6,100 feet
Management: Gila National Forest, Wilderness Ranger District; (575) 536-2250
Reservations: None
Activities: Hiking, fishing, and horseback riding
Season: Year-round
Finding the campground: From Silver City travel 20 miles north on NM 15 and then 5 miles east on NM 35 to the campground.
About the campground: This is another site with access to Lake Roberts. It makes an ideal base camp for enjoying all that the Gila has to offer. From here it's a short drive to the cliff dwellings or to trailheads into the wilderness. Riding stables are located nearby.

115 Scorpion

Location: 4 miles north of Gila Hot Springs
GPS: N33 13.811' / W108 15.455'
Sites: 10 sites for tents and RVs
Facilities: Vault toilets, tables, grills, and drinking water
Fee: None
Elevation: 5,700 feet
Management: Gila National Forest, Wilderness Ranger District; (575) 536-2250
Reservations: None
Activities: Hiking and fishing
Season: May through October
Finding the campground: From Gila Hot Springs travel 4 miles north on NM 15 to the campground.
About the campground: These 10 sites provide easy access to the cliff dwellings, hiking trails, and the river. The setting is peaceful, with sites shaded by cottonwoods.

116 Upper Black Canyon

Location: 22 miles north of Mimbres
GPS: N33 11.121' / W108 01.986'
Sites: 2 sites for tents and RVs
Facilities: Vault toilets, tables, grills, and drinking water
Fee: $
Elevation: 6,700 feet
Management: Gila National Forest, Wilderness Ranger District; (575) 536-2250
Reservations: None
Activities: Hiking and fishing
Season: May through October
Finding the campground: From Mimbres travel 10 miles northwest on NM 35. Turn north onto FR 150 and go 13.5 miles to the campground road. Turn west into the campground.
About the campground: Upper Black Canyon offers just one more opportunity to hide yourself away in the Gila. With only two sites here, the likelihood of crossing the path of another person is small. Just bring a comfortable lawn chair and enjoy.

117 Upper End

Location: 24 miles northeast of Silver City
GPS: N33 01.671' / W108 09.119'
Sites: 10 sites for tents

Mountain views and hiking draw campers to the Gila Wilderness Area.

Facilities: Vault toilets, tables, grills, and drinking water
Fee: $
Elevation: 6,100 feet
Management: Gila National Forest, Wilderness Ranger District; (575) 536-2250
Reservations: None
Activities: Hiking, fishing, and boating
Season: May through October
Finding the campground: From Silver City travel 20 miles north on NM 15 and then 4 miles east on NM 35 to the campground.
About the campground: Upper End is set among the ponderosa pines and oaks near Lake Roberts. The sites are nicely spaced for privacy, and this campground isn't as likely to fill on weekends as the two camps directly on the lake.

Deming–Las Cruces

The area between and around Deming and Las Cruces is one of the most desolate parts of the state, but it has its own brand of rugged beauty. From agate collecting and rock climbing at the state parks to attending some of the state's best rock concerts at New Mexico State University, there's no shortage of things to do in the area. The diversity found here is best exhibited by the contrast between the tiny hamlet of Hatch, with its nationally renowned chile crop, and the White Sands Missile Range, with its array of scientific partners and guests.

Camping here is not for the faint of heart or for those seeking the gentle beauty of pine-covered mountains. Come here looking for a challenge, both physical and mental, and you won't leave disappointed.

For more information:
Deming Chamber of Commerce
PO Box 8103 E. Ash St.
Deming, NM 88031
(575) 546-2674
www.demingchamber.com

Las Cruces Chamber of Commerce
505 S. Main St., Ste. 134
Las Cruces, NM 88001
(575) 524-1968
www.lascruces.org

Hatch Chamber of Commerce
PO Box 568
Hatch, NM 87937
(575) 519-4723
www.villageofhatch.org

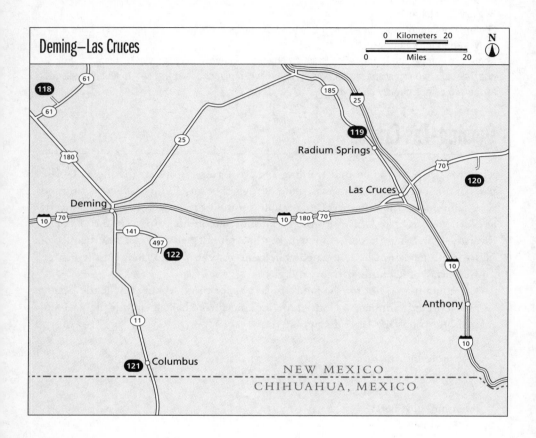

Deming–Las Cruces

118 City of Rocks State Park

Location: 28 miles northeast of Deming
GPS: N32 35.226' / W107 58.440'
Sites: 52 sites for tents and RVs
Facilities: Flush toilets, tables, grills, drinking water, visitor center, electricity, showers, and hiking trails
Fee: $ to $$, annual permit available
Elevation: 5,200 feet
Management: New Mexico State Parks Department; (575) 536-2800; www.emnrd.state.nm.us/SPD/cityofrocksstatepark.html

	Group sites	RV sites	Total # of sites	Max. RV length	Hookups	Toilets	Showers	Drinking water	Dump station	Pets	Wheelchair	Recreation	Fee	Season	Can reserve	Stay limit
118 City of Rocks State Park	•		52		WE	F		•	•		•	H	$-$$		•	14
119 Leasburg Dam State Park	•		31		WE	F		•	•	•	•	BHF	$-$$		•	14
120 Organ Mountains			D			V		•		•	•	HR				14
121 Pancho Villa State Park	•	•	79		WE	F		•	•	•		H	$-$$			14
122 Rockhound State Park	•	•	29		WE	F		•	•	•		H	$-$$			14

Hookups: W = Water,   E = Electric,   S = Sewer

Toilets: F = Flush,   V = Vault,   P = Pit,   C = Chemical

Recreation: H = Hiking,   S = Swimming,   F = Fishing,   B = Boating,   L = Boat Launch,   O = Off-Highway Driving,
   R = Horseback Riding

Fee (per-night campsite cost): $ = $0 to $5; $$ = $6 to $10; $$$ = $11 to $20.

Maximum Trailer/RV length given in feet. Stay limit given in days. If no entry under Maximum RV length where RV sites are
   available, no restriction is in place.

If no entry under Season, campground is open all year. If no entry under Fee, camping is free.

Reservations: Call (877) 664-7787; http://newmexicostateparks.reserveamerica.com

Activities: Hiking

Season: Year-round

Finding the campground: From Deming travel 23 miles northwest on US 180. Turn east onto NM 61 and go 3 miles to the park access road. Turn north and go 1.7 miles to the visitor center.

About the campground: Begin your journey through New Mexico's almost forgotten region by enjoying the unusual rock formations at City of Rocks. The towers are carved from layers of volcanic ash weathered by wind and water. The campground puts you right in the heart of the park so you can enjoy the scenery. Just don't expect much in the way of creature comforts, like shade. Only 10 of the sites have electricity, so even the cool of an air conditioner will be hard to come by here.

119 Leasburg Dam State Park

Location: 15 miles north of Las Cruces

GPS: N32 29.765' / W106 55.234'

Sites: 31 sites for tents and RVs

Facilities: Flush toilets, tables, grills, drinking water, visitor center, group sites, electricity, dump station, showers, playground, and hiking trails; wheelchair-accessible facilities

Fee: $ to $$, annual permit available
Elevation: 4,200 feet
Management: New Mexico State Parks Department; (575) 524-4068; www.emnrd.state.nm.us/SPD/leasburgdamstatepark.html
Reservations: Call (877) 664-7787; http://newmexicostateparks.reserveamerica.com
Activities: Hiking, fishing, waterskiing, sailing, and windsurfing
Season: Year-round
Finding the campground: From Las Cruces travel 15 miles north on NM 185 to Radium Springs and then follow the signs to the park.
About the campground: The oasis created by the Leasburg diversion dam is a cool retreat from the desert. The park offers canoeing and kayaking in addition to fishing and floating. Bring an inner tube.

120 Organ Mountains Recreation Area

Location: 20 miles east of Las Cruces
GPS: N32 22.153' / W106 33.672'
Sites: Dispersed
Facilities: Vault toilets, tables, grills, drinking water, and visitor center; wheelchair-accessible facilities
Fee: None
Elevation: 5,700 feet
Management: Bureau of Land Management–Mimbres Office; (575) 525-4300; www.blm.gov/nm
Reservations: None
Activities: Hiking and horseback riding
Season: Year-round
Finding the campground: From Las Cruces travel east 17 miles on US 70. Turn south on Dripping Springs Road and follow the signs about 3 miles to the campground.
About the campground: If you've ever looked at jagged desert mountains and wondered what camping in such a harsh place would be like, here's your opportunity. Campgrounds in the Organ Mountains have all the usual Bureau of Land Management amenities, and you can enjoy the rugged beauty of these high, desert peaks.

121 Pancho Villa State Park

Location: 35 miles south of Deming
GPS: N31 49.630' / W107 38.579'
Sites: 79 sites for tents and RVs
Facilities: Flush toilets, tables, grills, drinking water, visitor center, group sites, electricity, showers, playground, and hiking trails
Fee: $ to $$, annual permit available
Elevation: 4,000 feet

Management: New Mexico State Parks Department; (575) 531-2711; www.emnrd.state.nm.us/
SPD/panchovillastatepark.html
Reservations: None
Activities: Hiking and scenic driving
Season: Year-round
Finding the campground: From Deming travel 32 miles south on NM 11 to the park.
About the campground: There's no other place in New Mexico quite like Pancho Villa State Park.
Picture cactus so dense that only the roads, trails, trailer parking pads, and picnic tables remain
free of their prickly dominance. More than thirty varieties thrive here. The best time to visit is late
spring when the cacti explode with colorful blooms.

The other interesting feature here is the history. The park marks the last time mainland Amer-
ica was invaded by a foreign power. General Pancho Villa (a leader of the Mexican Revolution)
attacked the US Army post at Columbus in March 1916. In defense, the US Army used air power
and mechanized vehicles—the first time such tools were employed by the US military.

122 Rockhound State Park

Location: 14 miles southeast of Deming
GPS: N32 11.155' / W107 36.736'
Sites: 29 sites for tents and RVs
Facilities: Flush toilets, tables, grills, drinking water, visitor center, group sites, electricity, dump
station, showers, playground, and hiking trails
Fee: $ to $$, annual permit available
Elevation: 4,500 feet
Management: New Mexico State Parks Department; (575) 546-6182; www.emnrd.state.nm.us/
SPD/rockhoundstatepark.html
Reservations: None
Activities: Hiking and rock collecting
Season: Year-round
Finding the campground: From Deming travel 5 miles south on NM 11. Turn east onto NM 141
and go 6 miles. Turn southeast onto NM 497 and follow the signs to the park.
About the campground: Plenty has been said about the beautiful agate and flint specimens
found at this state park. It is unique in that it is the only state park that actually encourages visitors to gather rocks. Unfortunately, unless you are an expert rock climber, you aren't likely to find
much more than slivers that may have been washed out of the mountains by spring rains. The
prize pieces are found around 700 feet up in the jagged hills. The good news is that there is a rock
shop just outside the park entrance where you can purchase examples of what you could not find
for yourself.

There's also not much here in the way of creature comforts, like shade. There's no escaping
the fact that this is harsh country.

Alamogordo-Carrizozo-Cloudcroft

A 30-minute drive can take you from harsh desert to cool, pine-covered mountains. Of course, that's true in other places in the state, but the contrast is even greater here. At the foot of the Sacramento Mountains lies the White Sands National Monument. In spring you can romp in snow-white sand in one hour and in real snow the next. A little farther north another contrast exists in the Malpais lava beds, where you can camp atop bare lava rock one night and retreat into the aspens the next.

For more information:
Alamogordo Chamber of Commerce
1301 N. White Sands Blvd.
Alamogordo, NM 88310
(575) 437-6120 or (800) 826-0294
www.alamogordo.com

Carrizozo Chamber of Commerce
PO Box 567
Carrizozo, NM 88301
(575) 648-2732
www.carrizozochamber.org

Cloudcroft Chamber of Commerce
PO Box 1290
Cloudcroft, NM 88317
(575) 682-2733
www.coolcloudcroft.com

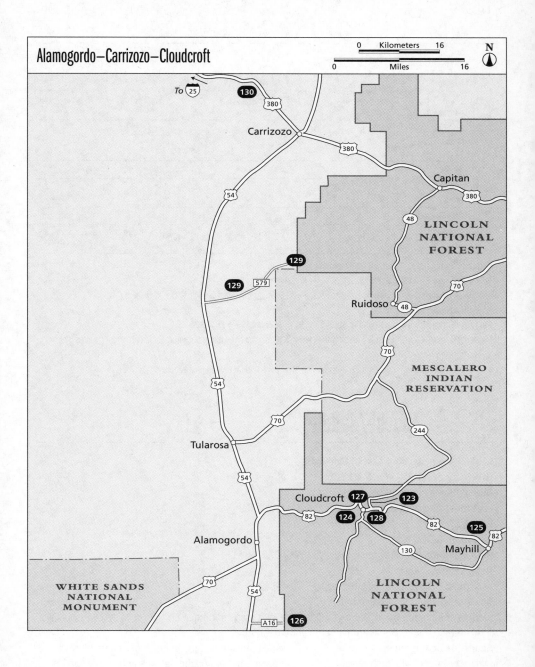

Alamogordo–Carrizozo–Cloudcroft

0 Kilometers 16

0 Miles 16

N

To 25 **130** 380

Carrizozo

380

Capitan

380

48 **LINCOLN NATIONAL FOREST**

54

129 579 **129**

70

Ruidoso 48

70

MESCALERO INDIAN RESERVATION

54

244

70

Tularosa

54

Cloudcroft **127** **123**

82 **124** **128** 82 **125** 82

Alamogordo 130 Mayhill

LINCOLN NATIONAL FOREST

70

54

WHITE SANDS NATIONAL MONUMENT

A16 **126**

	Group sites	RV sites	Total # of sites	Max. RV length	Hookups	Toilets	Showers	Drinking water	Dump station	Pets	Wheelchair	Recreation	Fee	Season	Can reserve	Stay limit
123	Apache/ Saddle		40			V		·		·		H	$	May–Sept		14
124	Deerhead	·	35			V		·		·		H	$$	May–Oct		14
125	James Canyon	·	5	16		V				·		H		Apr–Nov		14
126	Oliver Lee Memorial SP	·	44		WE	F	·	·	·	·	·	H	$–$$		·	14
127	Silver	·	32			V		·		·		H	$$	May–Nov		14
128	Sleepy Grass	·	45	16		V		·				HF	$$	May–Oct		14
129	Three Rivers	·	12			V		·		·		HR	$			14
130	Valley of Fires	·	12		E	V		·		·	·	H	$$			14

Hookups: W = Water,   E = Electric,   S = Sewer

Toilets: F = Flush,   V = Vault,   P = Pit,   C = Chemical

Recreation: H = Hiking,   S = Swimming,   F = Fishing,   B = Boating,   L = Boat Launch,   O = Off-Highway Driving,
   R = Horseback Riding

Fee (per-night campsite cost): $ = $0 to $5; $$ = $6 to $10; $$$ = $11 to $20.

Maximum Trailer/RV length given in feet. Stay limit given in days. If no entry under Maximum RV length where RV sites are
   available, no restriction is in place.

If no entry under Season, campground is open all year. If no entry under Fee, camping is free.

123 Apache/Saddle

Location: 3 miles northeast of Cloudcroft
GPS: N32 58.239' / W105 43.565'
Sites: 40 sites for tents and RVs
Facilities: Vault toilets, tables, grills, and drinking water
Fee: $
Elevation: 8,900 feet
Management: Lincoln National Forest; (575) 682-2551
Reservations: None
Activities: Hiking and scenic driving
Season: May through September
Finding the campground: From Cloudcroft travel 3 miles northeast on NM Highway 244 to FS24.
Turn south and go 0.5 mile to the campground entrance.
About the campground: Apache is one of several roadside campgrounds near Cloudcroft that
allow you to enjoy the lush forests of pine and aspen. The atmosphere is hushed, even when the
crowds move in on weekends.

124 Deerhead

Location: 1 mile south of Cloudcroft
GPS: N32 56.622' / W105 44.782'
Sites: 35 sites for tents and RVs
Facilities: Vault toilets, tables, grills, and drinking water
Fee: $$
Elevation: 8,700 feet
Management: Lincoln National Forest; (575) 682-2551
Reservations: None
Activities: Hiking and scenic driving
Season: May through October
Finding the campground: From Cloudcroft travel south 1 mile on NM 130 to the campground.
About the campground: Deerhead is located at the trailhead of the 21-mile Rim Trail, but the camp isn't overflowing with serious hikers. Perhaps a 21-mile hike is a bit too serious. The primary visitors here are West Texans looking for a place to escape the heat. The campground is lovely and designed to allow plenty of space for everyone.

125 James Canyon

Location: 2 miles northwest of Mayhill
GPS: N32 54.272' / W105 30.282'
Sites: 5 sites for tents and RVs
Facilities: Vault toilets, tables, and grills
Fee: None
Elevation: 6,800 feet
Management: Lincoln National Forest; (575) 682-2551
Reservations: None
Activities: Hiking and scenic driving
Season: April through November
Finding the campground: From Mayhill travel north on US 82 to the campground.
About the campground: There are no streams to fish here, no trails to hike, just a pretty pine forest to soothe away your troubles. Snag one of these five sites for a relaxing getaway.

126 Oliver Lee Memorial State Park

Location: 10 miles south of Alamogordo
GPS: N32 44.877' / W105 54.927'
Sites: 44 sites for tents and RVs
Facilities: Flush toilets, tables, grills, drinking water, visitor center, electricity, dump station, showers, and hiking trails; wheelchair-accessible facilities

Fee: $ to $$, annual permit available
Elevation: 4,300 feet
Management: New Mexico State Parks Department; (575) 437-8284; www.emnrd.state.nm.us/SPD/oliverleestatepark.html
Reservations: Call (877) 664-7787; http://newmexicostateparks.reserveamerica.com
Activities: Hiking
Season: Year-round
Finding the campground: In Alamogordo travel south on US 54 8.5 miles to the park entrance road A16. Turn east and go 4.25 miles to the visitor center.
About the campground: Oliver Lee is another of New Mexico's state parks that marks a historical landmark. In this case it's the ranch of Oliver Milton Lee, one of the state's most colorful founders. The nice thing about these historical parks is that the state works hard at making them pleasant retreats for visitors. Oliver Lee is no exception. The surrounding area may be harsh, but parts of the park are lovely and green most of the year due to the waters of Dog Canyon Creek. Most of the campsites have sheltered picnic tables, providing much-needed shade; many have electricity.

127 Silver

Location: 3 miles northeast of Cloudcroft
GPS: N32 58.465' / W105 43.585'
Sites: 32 sites for tents and RVs
Facilities: Vault toilets, tables, grills, drinking water, and showers
Fee: $$
Elevation: 9,000 feet
Management: Lincoln National Forest; (575) 682-2551
Reservations: None
Activities: Hiking
Season: May through November
Finding the campground: From Cloudcroft travel 3 miles north on NM 244 to FS24. Turn south and go 0.25 mile to the campground.
About the campground: Anglers will find it difficult to believe that so many campgrounds near Cloudcroft stay so full, since none of them have fishing access. If the lack of trout doesn't bother you, come on up. The pines and aspen are waiting. Silver has an overflow area, which is nothing more than a gravel parking lot, but you'll appreciate it if you have to arrive late on the weekend—at least it's camping.

128 Sleepy Grass

Location: 1.5 miles south of Cloudcroft
GPS: N32 56.407' / W105 44.436'
Sites: 45 sites for tents and RVs

Facilities: Vault toilets, tables, grills, and drinking water
Fee: $$
Elevation: 9,100 feet
Management: Lincoln National Forest; (575) 682-2551
Reservations: None
Activities: Hiking and fishing
Season: May through October
Finding the campground: From Cloudcroft travel 1 mile south on NM 130 to FR 24B/Apache Canyon Road. Turn east and go about 0.5 mile to the campground.
About the campground: The advantage this camp has over others in the Cloudcroft area is that it is just a bit off the road. That means two things—less traffic noise and fewer people. Unfortunately, the campground still fills on most summer weekends, so come early and ask the rangers to put this beautiful camp on the reservation system.

129 Three Rivers/Three Rivers Petroglyph National Recreation Site

Location: 30 miles south of Carrizozo
GPS: N33 24.064' / W105 53.2235'
Sites: 12 sites for tents and RVs
Facilities: Vault toilets, tables, drinking water, and corrals
Fee: $
Elevation: 5,000 to 6,800 feet
Management: Bureau of Land Management, Caballo Field Office; (575) 525-4300; and Lincoln National Forest, Smokey Bear Ranger District; (575) 257-4095
Reservations: None
Activities: Hiking and horseback riding
Season: Year-round
Finding the campground: From Carrizozo travel 25 miles south on US 54. Turn east onto FR 579 and go 4.5 miles to the petroglyph site and another 8.5 miles to the Three Rivers campground.
About the campgrounds: There are camping facilities at the petroglyph site and at the edge of the White Mountain Wilderness. Both sites are situated in grasslands, with stunning views of the mountains to the east and the desert floor to the west. The national forest site is designed for horse campers, with trails leading into the wilderness area.

130 Valley of Fires Recreation Area

Location: 4 miles west of Carrizozo
GPS: N33 40.946' / W105 55.335'
Sites: 12 sites for tents and RVs
Facilities: Vault toilets, tables, grills, drinking water, and electricity; wheelchair-accessible facilities

Fee: $$
Elevation: 5,100 feet
Management: National Park Service; (575) 887-2241
Reservations: None
Activities: Hiking
Season: Year-round
Finding the campground: From Carrizozo travel 4 miles west on US 380 to the campground access road.
About the campground: Valley of Fires is for those looking for a camping experience that's a bit out of the ordinary. The campground sits atop the most recent lava flow in the continental United States. The experience is fascinating for natural science lovers. The lava beds are a wildlife habitat all their own. Even the squirrels that live on the flow are a different color than those living on the surrounding desert floor.

Southeast

Throughout most of this quadrant of the state, the mountains are still a faint blue line teasing the horizon. But the rugged foothills hold a beauty all their own. There are jewels in the desert, like Carlsbad and Roswell.

The mountains break the rolling plains at the far western edge of the region. Summer and winter playgrounds at Ruidoso are the big attractions. Campgrounds are plentiful, as well as beautiful.

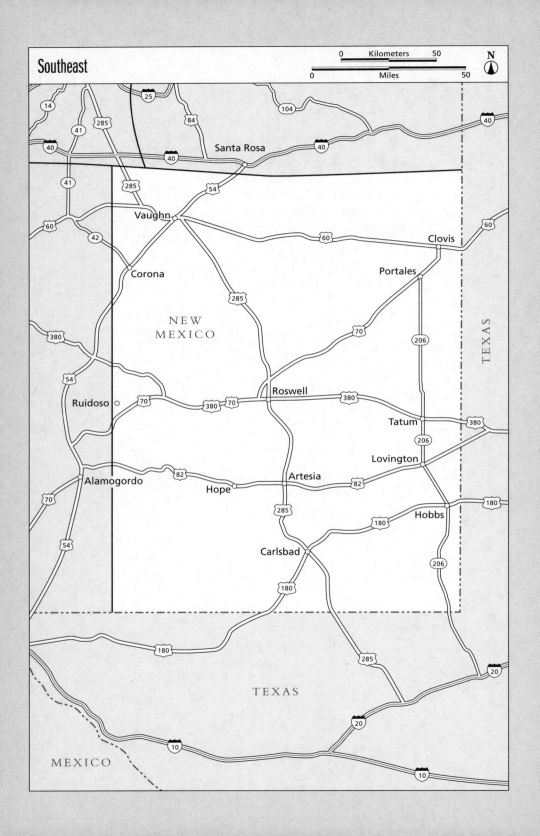

Clovis-Portales

These two towns are gateways between Texas and New Mexico. They have a bit more in common with their Texas neighbors than with the rest of New Mexico. Agriculture (primarily cattle and dairy) provides the mainstay of both communities. Neither town is without some New Mexican charm, however. You just have to look past the Texas influences.

For more information:
Clovis Chamber of Commerce
105 E. Grand Ave.
Clovis, NM 88101
(800) 261-7656
www.clovisnm.org

Portales/Roosevelt County Chamber of Commerce
100 S. Avenue A
Portales, NM 88130
(575) 356-8541 or (800) 635-8036
www.portales.com

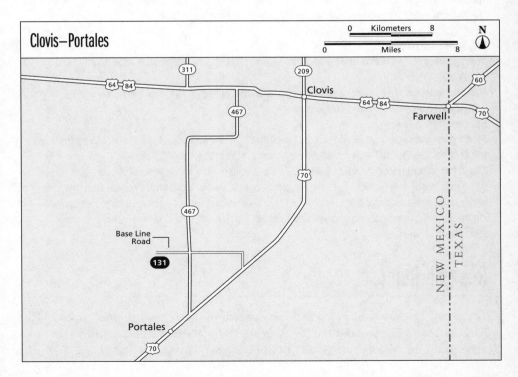

	Group sites	RV sites	Total # of sites	Max. RV length	Hookups	Toilets	Showers	Drinking water	Dump station	Pets	Wheelchair	Recreation	Fee	Season	Can reserve	Stay limit
131	Oasis State Park		·	23		WE	FV	·	·	·	·	·	HF	$-$$		·	14

Hookups: W = Water, E = Electric, S = Sewer
Toilets: F = Flush, V = Vault, P = Pit, C = Chemical
Recreation: H = Hiking, S = Swimming, F = Fishing, B = Boating, L = Boat Launch, O = Off-Highway Driving,
  R = Horseback Riding
Fee (per-night campsite cost): $ = $0 to $5; $$ = $6 to $10; $$$ = $11 to $20.
Maximum Trailer/RV length given in feet. Stay limit given in days. If no entry under Maximum RV length where RV sites are
  available, no restriction is in place.
If no entry under Season, campground is open all year. If no entry under Fee, camping is free.

131 Oasis State Park

Location: 7 miles north of Portales
GPS: N34 15.588' / W103 20.996'
Sites: 23 sites for tents and RVs, 13 with electricity
Facilities: Vault and flush toilets, tables, grills, some shelters, showers, some electrical hookups, playground, water, dump station, and trails; wheelchair-accessible facilities
Fee: $ to $$, annual permit available
Elevation: 4,010 feet
Management: New Mexico State Parks Department; (575) 356-5331; www.emnrd.state.nm.us/SPD/oasisstatepark.html
Reservations: Call (877) 664-7787; http://newmexicostateparks.reserveamerica.com
Activities: Hiking, fishing, and bird watching
Season: Year-round
Finding the campground: From Portales travel north on NM 467 about 6 miles to the park access road (Base Line Road). Turn west and drive about 1 mile to the park.
About the campground: This interesting little state park makes a wonderful stopover point as you travel into or out of New Mexico. There are plenty of cottonwoods to provide respite from the sun and a quiet pond for fishing. You won't find the park crowded except perhaps with locals picnicking on Sunday afternoons. Birders will find the spot ideal, as the pond is winter home to more than 80 different species.

Roswell–Ruidoso

These two cities are connected by a long stretch of lonely road and not much else. Roswell is an oil town and the home of the New Mexico Military Institute. Two museums document Roswell's UFO claim to fame. Ruidoso is the playground in

Roswell—Ruidoso

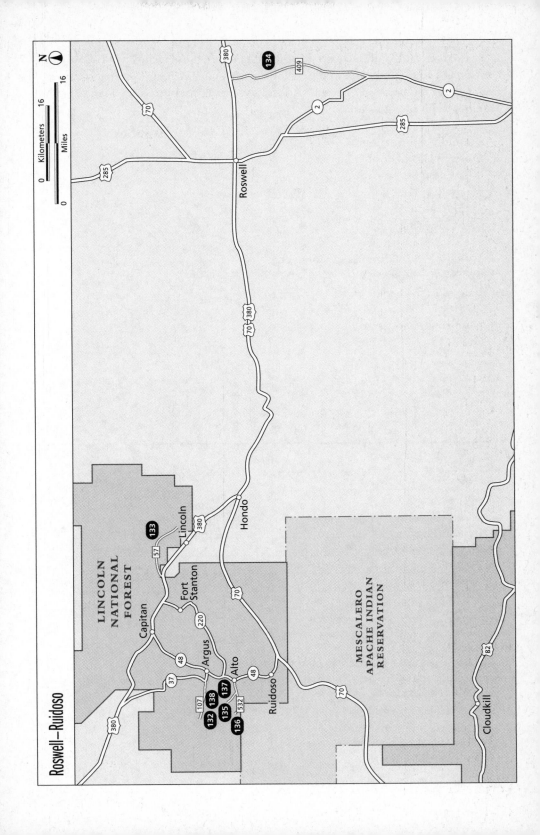

Roswell's backyard. With such attractions as a ski resort, horse racing, world-class golf courses, and access to the beautiful Sierra Blanca Mountains, Ruidoso attracts visitors from all over southeastern New Mexico and western Texas. Both cities boast enough activities to fill a long weekend.

For more information:
Roswell Chamber of Commerce
131 W. 2nd St.
Roswell, NM 88201
(575) 623-5695
www.roswellnm.org

Ruidoso Valley Chamber of Commerce
720 Sudderth Dr.
Ruidoso, NM 88345
(575) 257-7395
www.ruidosonow.com

		Group sites	RV sites	Total # of sites	Max. RV length	Hookups	Toilets	Showers	Drinking water	Dump station	Pets	Wheelchair	Recreation	Fee	Season	Can reserve	Stay limit
132	Argentina-Bonito		·	D			V				·		HR	$	May–Oct		14
133	Baca	·		D			V				·		H		May–Oct		14
134	Bottomless Lakes SP		·	37		WE	F	·	·	·	·	·	HFSB	$–$$		·	14
135	Monjeau			12			V				·		H	$	May–Oct		14
136	Oak Grove		·	29	18		V				·		H	$	May–Oct		14
137	Skyline		·	17			V				·		H	$	May–Oct		14
138	Southfork		·	60	20		V	·		·	·		HF	$$	May–Oct		14

Hookups: W = Water,   E = Electric,   S = Sewer
Toilets: F = Flush,   V = Vault,   P = Pit,   C = Chemical
Recreation: H = Hiking,   S = Swimming,   F = Fishing,   B = Boating,   L = Boat Launch,   O = Off-Highway Driving,
    R = Horseback Riding
Fee (per-night campsite cost): $ = $0 to $5; $$ = $6 to $10; $$$ = $11 to $20.
Maximum Trailer/RV length given in feet. Stay limit given in days. If no entry under Maximum RV length where RV sites are
    available, no restriction is in place.
If no entry under Season, campground is open all year. If no entry under Fee, camping is free.

Campgrounds in the Ruidoso area are spacious enough for big rigs.
SALLY JOHNSON

132 Argentina-Bonito

Location: 18 miles northwest of Ruidoso
GPS: N33 27.804' / W105 48.276'
Sites: Dispersed
Facilities: Vault toilets
Fee: $

Elevation: 7,600 feet
Management: Lincoln National Forest, Smokey Bear Ranger District; (575) 257-4095
Reservations: None
Activities: Hiking and horseback riding
Season: May through October
Finding the campground: From Ruidoso travel 10 miles north on NM 48. Turn west on FR 107 and go 8 miles to the campground.
About the campground: Argentina-Bonito is not really a formal campground, but rather an area for primitive horseback camping; expect heavy use, especially during fall hunting seasons. The aspens and miles of trails and mining roads to explore are the main attractions for most equestrians.

133 Baca

Location: 17 miles east of Capitan
GPS: N33 32.355' / W105 21.549'
Sites: Dispersed
Facilities: Vault toilets
Fee: None
Elevation: 7,200 feet
Management: Lincoln National Forest, Smokey Bear Ranger District; (575) 257-4095
Reservations: None
Activities: Hiking
Season: May through October
Finding the campground: From Capitan travel 8 miles east on US 380. Turn north onto FR 57 and go 9 miles to the campground.
About the campground: Tenters and people with small trailers might find that this is the perfect spot during summer months if they're just looking for a mountain getaway. There's not much to do here but kick back and relax. The advantage is that you might have the place all to yourself.

134 Bottomless Lakes State Park

Location: 16 miles southeast of Roswell
GPS: N33 20.316' / W104 20.144'
Sites: 37 sites for tents and RVs
Facilities: Flush toilets, tables, grills, drinking water, visitor center, group sites, electricity, dump station, showers, playground, and hiking trails; wheelchair-accessible facilities
Fee: $ to $$, annual permit available
Elevation: 3,500 feet
Management: New Mexico State Parks Department; (575) 624-6058; www.emnrd.state.nm.us/SPD/bottomlesslakesstatepark.html
Reservations: Call (877) 664-7787; http://newmexicostateparks.reserveamerica.com

Activities: Hiking, swimming, fishing, and boating

Season: Year-round

Finding the campground: From Roswell travel 10 miles east on US 380. Turn south onto NM 409 and go 3.1 miles to the park entrance.

About the campground: Bottomless Lakes is another example of how the New Mexico state park system showcases the oddities of the state and combines them with recreational opportunities when it can. The lakes here are really sinkholes ranging in depth from 17 to 90 feet. Some are clear enough to attract scuba divers, but most are a murky, blue-green color. The camping facilities make this a nice stopover or a good point from which to enjoy the attractions in Roswell.

135 Monjeau

Location: 11 miles northwest of Ruidoso

GPS: N33 25.921' / W105 43.799'

Sites: 12 sites for tents

Facilities: Vault toilets, tables, and grills

Fee: $

Elevation: 7,600 feet

Management: Lincoln National Forest, Smokey Bear Ranger District; (575) 257-4095

Reservations: None

Activities: Hiking

Season: May through October

Finding the campground: From Ruidoso travel 5 miles north on NM 48. Turn west onto FR 127/ NM 532 and go 1 mile. Turn north on FR 117 and go 5 miles to the campground.

About the campground: Monjeau is one of the prettiest campgrounds in the Lincoln National Forest. The camp was once a fire lookout. The only thing missing is a stream full of trout.

136 Oak Grove

Location: 9 miles northwest of Ruidoso

GPS: N33 23.771' / W105 44.799'

Sites: 29 sites for tents and RVs

Facilities: Vault toilets, tables, and grills

Fee: $

Elevation: 8,400 feet

Management: Lincoln National Forest, Smokey Bear Ranger District; (575) 257-4095

Reservations: None

Activities: Hiking

Season: May through October

Finding the campground: From Ruidoso travel 5 miles north on NM 48. Turn west onto FR 127/ NM 532 and go 4 miles to the campground.

About the campground: Oak Grove lives up to its name, as it sits in a mixed oak and aspen forest on the road to the Ski Apache resort. The 29 sites here will fill quickly in summer, and unfortunately, this camp isn't on the reservation system. You'd be wise to arrive early or have an alternate plan.

137 Skyline

Location: 10 miles northwest of Ruidoso
GPS: N33 25.205' / W105 44.066'
Sites: 17 sites for tents and RVs
Facilities: Vault toilets, tables, and grills
Fee: $
Elevation: 7,400 feet
Management: Lincoln National Forest, Smokey Bear Ranger District; (575) 257-4095
Reservations: None
Activities: Hiking
Season: May through October
Finding the campground: From Ruidoso travel 5 miles north on NM 48. Turn west onto FR 127/ NM 532 and go 1 mile. Turn north on FR 117 and go 4 miles to the campground.
About the campground: Skyline is a camp for lovers of windswept, wide-open spaces. From this high perch you can hike above the timberline and enjoy the vistas in all directions. "Breathtaking" doesn't even come close to describing the views found here.

138 Southfork

Location: 14 miles northwest of Ruidoso
GPS: N33 26.945' / W105 45.194'
Sites: 60 sites for tents and RVs
Facilities: Vault toilets, tables, grills, and drinking water; wheelchair-accessible facilities
Fee: $$
Elevation: 7,500 feet
Management: Lincoln National Forest, Smokey Bear Ranger District; (575) 257-4095
Reservations: None
Activities: Hiking and fishing
Season: May through October
Finding the campground: From Ruidoso travel 10 miles north on NM 48. Turn west on FR 107 and go 4 miles to the campground.
About the campground: Southfork is no longer on the National Recreation Reservation System, but it should be. This is the most popular campground in the Ruidoso area, and even though it's the largest, spaces fill very early on summer weekends. The big draw here is access to the shore of Bonito Lake. The crystal-clear waters are well stocked, and fishing is usually excellent.

The campground itself is not well designed. Spaces are crowded together; many are side-by-side, parking-lot style. Having said all that, it's still a nice place to camp if you want to fish. Try a weekday visit to avoid the crowds.

Lovington-Hobbs-Artesia-Carlsbad

This is oil country. There are probably more pump jacks than people per square mile in this desolate region. With the exception of Carlsbad, these communities have little to attract visitors. Those who do come through are often surprised by what they find. The people are friendly and the food is good.

As for Carlsbad, the Carlsbad Caverns National Park is the big attraction. And rightly so. The park service works very hard to attract visitors by changing and upgrading its offerings. There is no public vehicle camping in or around Carlsbad Caverns National Park, so check with commercial RV parks for camping accommodations.

For more information:
Lovington Chamber of Commerce
201 S. Main Ave.
Lovington, NM 88260
(575) 396-5311
http://lovingtonchamber.org

Artesia Chamber of Commerce
107 N. First St.
Artesia, NM 88210
(575) 746-2744
www.artesiachamber.com

Hobbs Chamber of Commerce
400 N. Marland
Hobbs, NM 88240
(575) 397-3202
www.hobbschamber.org

Carlsbad Chamber of Commerce
302 S. Canal
Carlsbad, NM 88220
(575) 887-6516
www.carlsbadchamber.com

Carlsbad Caverns National Park
3225 National Parks Hwy.
Carlsbad, NM 88220
(575) 785-2232
www.nps.gov/cave

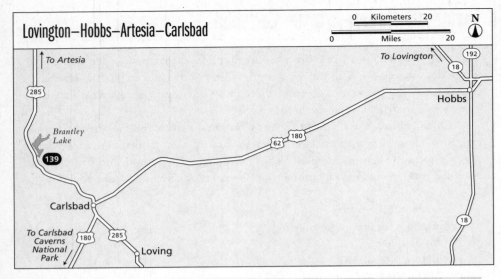

Lovington–Hobbs–Artesia–Carlsbad

	Group sites	RV sites	Total # of sites	Max. RV length	Hookups	Toilets	Showers	Drinking water	Dump station	Pets	Wheelchair	Recreation	Fee	Season	Can reserve	Stay limit
139 **Brantley Lake State Park**	·	·	51		WE	F	·	·	·	·	·	HFB	$–$$		·	14

Hookups: W = Water, E = Electric, S = Sewer

Toilets: F = Flush, V = Vault, P = Pit, C = Chemical

Recreation: H = Hiking, S = Swimming, F = Fishing, B = Boating, L = Boat Launch, O = Off-Highway Driving,
R = Horseback Riding

Fee (per-night campsite cost): $ = $0 to $5; $$ = $6 to $10; $$$ = $11 to $20.

Maximum Trailer/RV length given in feet. Stay limit given in days. If no entry under Maximum RV length where RV sites are available, no restriction is in place.

If no entry under Season, campground is open all year. If no entry under Fee, camping is free.

139 **Brantley Lake State Park**

Location: 12 miles north of Carlsbad

GPS: N32 34.104' / W104 22.493'

Sites: 51 sites for tents and RVs

Facilities: Flush toilets, tables, grills, drinking water, visitor center, group sites, electricity, dump station, showers, playground, and hiking trails; wheelchair-accessible facilities

Fee: $ to $$, annual permit available

Elevation: 3,300 feet

Management: New Mexico State Parks Department; (575) 457-2384; www.emnrd.state.nm.us/SPD/brantleylakestatepark.html

Reservations: Call (877) 664-7787; http://newmexicostateparks.reserveamerica.com
Activities: Hiking, fishing, boating, waterskiing, sailing, and windsurfing
Season: Year-round
Finding the campground: From Carlsbad travel 10 miles north on US 285. Turn east onto the park access road and go 2 miles to the park.
About the campground: When you live in the desert Southwest, you take every opportunity you can to get wet. Brantley Lake is one of those watering holes that attracts locals by the dozens. It does make a nice stopover or a good base camp for exploring all that Carlsbad has to offer.

The nightly flight of the bats at Carlsbad is a sight to behold.

Giant formations like this one are abundant in the main cave at Carlsbad Caverns National Park.

Index

About the Author

Camping New Mexico is Melinda Crow's fourth FalconGuide®. As an avid lifetime camper, and now as the owner of an RV resort in central Texas, Crow knows camping. Her own camping modes have ranged from tents to tent trailers, from pickup campers to plush RVs. Although she has camped across the entire southern United States, her favorite destinations are still found in New Mexico.

Other FalconGuides® written by Crow are *Camping Colorado, Rockhounding Texas,* and *The Rockhound's Guide to New Mexico.* Her magazine articles have appeared in *Texas Highways, 3-2-1 Contact, Parenting,* and *Family Fun.* She is a regular contributor to Yahoo! Travel.